50
E V E N   M O R E
UNUSUAL THINGS
TO SEE IN ONTARIO

50

EVEN MORE

UNUSUAL THINGS
TO SEE IN ONTARIO

RON BROWN

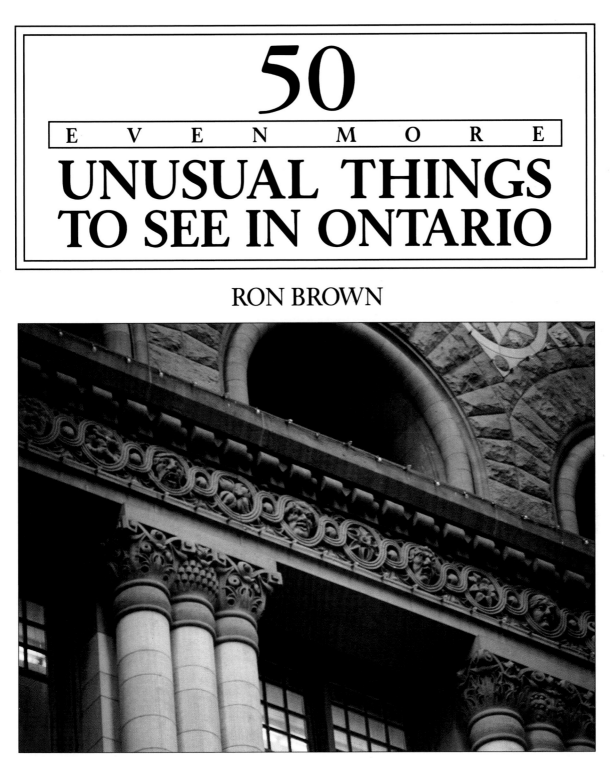

The faces of Old City Hall, Toronto.

A BOSTON MILLS PRESS BOOK

CANADIAN CATALOGUING IN PUBLICATION DATA

Brown, Ron, 1945-
Fifty even more unusual things to see in Ontario

ISBN 1-55046-057-9

1. Ontario - Guidebooks.   2. Curiosities and
wonders - Ontario - Guidebooks. I. Title.
II. Title: Fifty even more unusual things
to see in Ontario

FC3057.B76 1993   917.1304'4   C93-093605-1
F1057.B76 1993

03 02 01 00 99   3 4 5 6 7

Reprinted in 1999 by
BOSTON MILLS PRESS
132 Main Street
Erin, Ontario N0B 1T0
Tel 519-833-2407
Fax 519-833-2195
e-mail books@boston-mills.on.ca
www.boston-mills.on.ca

An affiliate of
STODDART PUBLISHING CO. LIMITED
34 Lesmill Road
Toronto, Ontario, Canada
M3B 2T6
Tel 416-445-3333
Fax 416-445-5967
e-mail gdsinc@genpub.com

Distributed in Canada by
General Distribution Services Limited
325 Humber College Boulevard
Toronto, Canada M9W 7C3
Orders 1-800-387-0141 Ontario & Quebec
Orders 1-800-387-0172 NW Ontario & Other Provinces
e-mail customer.service@ccmailgw.genpub.com
EDI Canadian Telebook S1150391

Distributed in the United States by
General Distribution Services Inc.
85 River Rock Drive, Suite 202
Buffalo, New York 14207-2170
1-800-805-1083
fax 1-800-481-6207
e-mail gdsinc@genpub.com
www.genpub.com
PUBNET 6307949

Design by Gillian Stead
Typesetting by Justified Type Inc., Guelph
Printed in Hong Kong by Book Art Inc., Toronto

The photograph that accompanies the story of White River was thoughtfully provided by Norm Jaehrling,
economic development officer for the Town of White River. All other photographs are by the author.

Contents

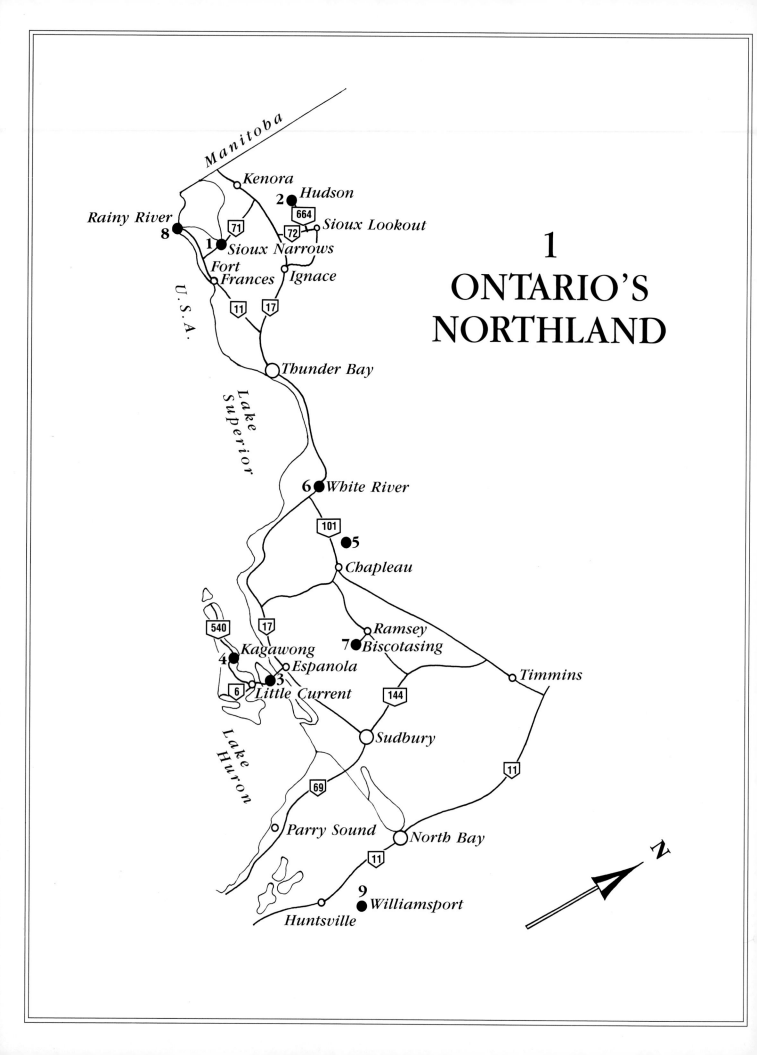

1
ONTARIO'S NORTHLAND

1
Over the Sioux Narrows:
North America's Longest Wooden Bridge

Sioux Narrows is an unlikely place to find the continent's biggest anything. A tiny tourist town of fewer than 400, Sioux Narrows straddles Highway 71 about 80 kilometres southeast of Kenora, Ontario. It also straddles Sioux Narrows, an intriguingly named channel of water along the eastern shore of the Lake of the Woods. Although traditionally the territory of the Cree, the Lake of the Woods was subjected to frequent raids by the western Sioux tribes. Key defensive locations such as Sioux Narrows often took on the name of the intruders. Sioux Lookout, farther north, is another.

In the 1920s the lumber camps in the area attracted "Europeans" who stayed and became settlers. With no railway the settlers relied on the Lake of the Woods and on a dirt trail to the south for transportation. In 1936 the Depression era road-building program brought highway links to both the north and the south. Only the Sioux Narrows on the Lake of the Woods stood in the way of a through route.

Using creosoted Douglas fir from British Columbia, the highway engineers bridged the chasm and in so doing inadvertently gave Sioux Narrows its unusual claim to fame — the longest single-span wooden bridge in North America. Its main span, the Howe Truss, covers 64 metres, and the bridge's total length is more than 110 metres. The record is proclaimed on a local plaque and through the bridge's designation by the Ontario government as a heritage site.

Located amid high granite cliffs that tower above the water and the pine trees that bend in the wind, North America's longest wooden bridge seems right at home.

North America's longest single-span wooden bridge extends over the Sioux Narrows.

2

Dry-Land Shipwrecks: Hudson's Boat Graveyard

When boats have outlived their usefulness, they are either cut up for scrap or sunk. At the remote northwestern Ontario town of Hudson, however, they were simply hauled up onto the shore and abandoned.

For 10 heady years Hudson was the jumping-off point for a spirited gold-and-silver rush to the Red Lake area. After the First World War Red Lake was known to few others than fur traders and a handful of adventurous prospectors. One was Lorne Howey, who in 1925 finally discovered what they had all been looking for — the telltale glitter of gold. The rush was on.

In 1926 prospectors staked more than 13,000 claims and in 1927 more than 15,000. The problem was how to get to Red Lake. The closest railway was the CNR, 290 kilometres to the south, and the closest community on that railway was Hudson. But there was Lac Seul. A long U-shaped lake, Lac Seul was an established water route for natives and fur traders and penetrated deep into the woodlands both to the northwest and northeast of Hudson. It was the ideal route to the gold fields, and prospectors poured off the trains at the rate of 40 a day.

Until the great rush, the only boats on the lake were the tugs of the small fishing companies and the pointers of the Hudson's Bay Company. The rush, however, created an enormous need for water transportation. William Leranger arrived from Quebec and built a number of barges. The Lac Seul Transport Company, the Triangle Fish Company and the Orsa Red Lake Line launched the *Prospector*, the *Triangle* and the *Triton* respectively, the latter capable of sleeping 15 passengers in cabins and an additional 35 on the deck.

Freight destined for the Pickle Lake gold fields to the northeast was portaged over a marine railway at Root Bay, while that bound for Red Lake to the

northwest had to cross four. Although air transportation existed, the water route remained cheaper than even the winter truck route. Talk of a railway to Red Lake ended when the federal government killed the proposed Red Lake & North Western Railway.

The Red Lake gold fields went on to spawn 15 producing mines, and the Lac Seul water highway remained busy with the sight of barges chugging slowly across the grey waters.

In 1947 a long-awaited highway was opened between the gold mines and the CNR at Red Lake Road, and the lengthy and awkward barge route fell into disuse.

Most of the old boats were hauled onto the shore 2 kilometres east of Hudson and forgotten. Timbers rotted and fell off; trees pushed their way up through the hulls. Although neither extensive nor highly visible, the Hudson boat graveyard remains an unusual monument to a short-lived but vital era in the growth of Ontario's northwest.

Hudson is a quieter place now that the trains no longer stop and the prospectors have gone elsewhere. Sioux Lookout has assumed the role of the most important town in the region. Most of the mines lie abandoned, only a handful having had the gold reserves to continue operating. While the old marine railways lie neglected, the Red Lake Road has been upgraded and become Highway 105. With its new access, Red Lake itself has been able to overcome its downturn with a tourist boom. None of the activity would have occurred, though, without Lac Seul's watery highway and the old boats that chugged along it.

The skeleton of an old schooner rests on the shore of Lac Seul.

3
The Devil's Ice Rink

The Manitoulin area, the spiritual homeland to thousands of Ontario's native people, is a place of not just legend and lore, but strange sights as well — the La Cloche Mountains, with their gleaming white rock, the vast panorama that spreads out from the 10 Mile Point Lookout, and the Devil's Ice Rink.

The huge limestone mesa that forms Manitoulin Island comprises hard layers of rock. Wherever a layer outcrops, its surface is level. Much of this limestone bedrock remains buried beneath old lake sediments or glacial debris. But along Highway 6, north of the attractive village of Little Current, lies a bare surface of limestone bedrock that is flat and clear, as if it were a stony ice rink.

An explanation of how it occurred also tells the story of Ontario's ice age. As the great ice sheets ground their way southward, they scraped clean the flat surfaces of the limestone. While other areas of rock were covered over with glacial debris, or with lake sediments, the bedrock north of Manitoulin remained near the surface of ancient post-glacial Lake Algonquin. The relentless waves of that lake kept the surface of the rocks washed clear and smooth.

Although this phenomenon is common in limestone areas throughout Ontario, nowhere can you witness such an extensive area as at the Devil's Ice Rink, another of Manitoulin's many wonders.

This flat limestone surface forms the Devil's Ice Rink near Little Current.

4

Kagawong: Ontario's Prettiest Village

Ontario is fortunate in that it contains some of North America's most attractive small communities. Still largely unspoiled by the roadside sprawl and downtown demolitions that have ruined small-town USA and now threaten the province, Ontario's villages and towns range from western-style boom towns like Rainy River to those with a strong maritime flavour like Snug Harbour. But to many, Kagawong, on Manitoulin Island's north shore, is simply the prettiest.

The white clapboard buildings in this one-time fishing village and steamer port stretch along the waters of Mudge Bay. In the early morning the buildings are reflected in the calm water, and behind them the wooded face of the limestone cliff provides a leafy backdrop. Across the harbour the once vacant shell of the former pulp mill now houses festivals and flea markets.

The most interesting of the village structures, the Anglican marine church, backs onto the water. Its unusual pulpit is made from the prow of a boat. Miniature fishing boats hang from the ends of the pews, and the stained-glass windows appropriately depict a ship and anchor. Such decor befits a town that once depended on the lake for its livelihood and its lifeline.

Kagawong offers other pleasures to explorers. Hikers can use the trail to nearby Bridal Veil Falls, more a delicate spray than a foaming cascade. Strollers can follow the walking-tour map of the village (available in most stores), and drivers can continue along the road to Maple Point, where a sweeping view takes in the waters and the islands of the North Channel.

The harbourside portion of the village is about 2 kilometres north of Highway 540 and about 40 kilometres west of Little Current.

The reflections of Kagawong.

5

Nicholson: A Ghost Town Worth Visiting

The province of Quebec can boast about its ghost-town park, Val Jalbert, and Michigan has Fayette, but Ontario only came close to having a ghost-town park.

Nicholson came into existence because of the vision of two determined entrepreneurs. Northerners James Austin and George Nicholson from Chapleau, a railway centre and the site of a sawmill, recognized the growing demand for timber to use as railway ties, so on the shore of Windermere Lake, about 19 kilometres west of Chapleau, they built a mill to manufacture ties. The bustling town, with two churches, a hotel, a store, a school and a boarding house, was for three decades home to 250 people. When the mill burned down in 1933, the town was largely abandoned.

Forty years later, a team of Ontario government historians visited the site. They parted the bushes and stared in amazement. Before them, overgrown and weathered, stood the gaunt ruins of the once-thriving town. The site so impressed them that they recommended Nicholson be developed as a ghost-town park.

That might have happened except for two things. First, the government department to which the historians reported was the Ministry of Natural Resources. Regarding the project as beyond its purview, the ministry ignored the recommendations. Then, shortly after the report was submitted, a careless hunter accidentally set one of the flimsy structures ablaze. The ensuing inferno consumed most of what had been the main street and, with it, Ontario's hopes of having a ghost-town park.

Despite the destruction, the site is one of the province's most picturesque. Several of the old cabins still stand, now in use as cottages. Smaller cabins and the schoolhouse are surrounded by forest. Most remarkable is the sagging wooden church, its slender steeple decidedly tilted and nearing collapse as nature encroaches.

Although it is possible to reach the site by train from Chapleau, schedules do not permit a same-day return. The simplest route to the site is by boat from Shoals Provincial Park, located on the south side of the lake.

Unless they are preserved, ghost towns don't last long, and this old gem is fading fast. If provincial government decision-makers had acted years ago, Ontario, too, could have had a ghost-town park.

The ghost town of Nicholson
almost became a ghost-town park.

6

Winnie the Pooh's Home Town: White River's New Claim to Fame

For years Canadians travelling the Trans-Canada Highway have paused in White River, Ontario, to photograph the thermometer that declares it the "coldest spot in Canada." (In reality the −72° recorded that bone-numbing night back in 1935 was an unofficial measurement. The lowest officially recorded temperature was −63° at Snag, Yukon Territories, on February 3, 1947.) Today, however, White River proudly proclaims its new status as the birthplace of Winnie the Pooh.

The story began in 1914 on the worn wooden platform of the barn-like CP railway station. Capt. Harry Colebourn, a Canadian Army veterinarian from Winnipeg, stepped from the troop train that was carrying him to Valcartier, Quebec. As he paced the platform waiting for the engine to be serviced, he noticed a hunter with a black bear cub.

Army officers commonly purchased such mascots for their regiments, so for $20 the cub became the property of the Canadian Army Veterinary Corps. The mascot needed a name, and Colebourn chose Winnipeg, after his home town.

In England the bear was an instant hit with the troops, who shortened the name to Winnie. During the First World War, Colebourn left Winnie with the London Zoo, where the bear became just as popular with the children as she had been with the soldiers. One child who fantasized the bear into his life was young Christopher Robin Milne, son of the writer A.A. Milne.

Winnie the Pooh now welcomes visitors to his home town of White River.
Courtesy of the Town of White River.

Literary history was made. A.A. Milne's Winnie the Pooh books captivated millions of children worldwide. Today the little bear enjoys even greater exposure, owing to the Disney Corporation, which now owns the rights to Winnie.

Tom Bagdon, a long-time White River resident and originator of the "coldest temperature" symbol, first proposed building a statue to celebrate the town's link with the world's most famous bear. Strangely, Disney at first had no desire to let White River commission a statue of the bear. However a letter-writing campaign softened the corporate giant's heart, and the statue was unveiled, with Disney representatives in attendance, in August 1992.

The 4.5-metre statue by sculptor George Barone depicts Winnie in a pose inspired by the original illustrator, Ernest H. Shepard, waving from a tree. Made of a material developed by Barone himself, using a mixture of marble dust and fibreglass resins (he calls it "marblite"), it beckons to Trans-Canada Highway travellers from the entrance to the visitors' park.

Here, too, you can learn the story of Winnie and, of course, purchase Winnie souvenirs.

Meanwhile, down by the station, the only passenger trains that stop these days are the silvery Budd cars that operate three times weekly between White River and Sudbury. And, yes, if you wish, you can still photograph the thermometer.

7

Biscotasing: Land of Grey Owl

White River is not the only northeastern community with a claim on a historic figure.

Biscotasing is something of a ghost town. Its population of about 50 permanent residents occupies a mix of new homes and old houses beside Biscotasi Lake on the CPR line some 150 kilometres northwest of Sudbury. And that's just as well, because when the only road, a narrow 38-kilometre dirt road from Ramsay, becomes impassable, as it often does, the only way in and out is by train.

And that was the only way nearly 90 years ago, when an Englishman named Archibald Stansfeld Belaney arrived, eager to learn about the aboriginal way of life that he had heard so much about in his native Hastings, England.

He was soon accepted into a local aboriginal band and married one of their number. His youthful years in Bisco, then a rowdy railway town, were full of fights and drunkenness, and shortly after becoming the main suspect in a stabbing, he left town.

Later, calling himself Grey Owl, he became a popular lecturer and a prolific writer on the subject of conservation. His ruse remained undiscovered until after his death in 1938. But despite Grey Owl's dubious celebrity status, Bisco residents, remembering "their" Archie, weren't in a hurry to proclaim their affiliation with him.

Biscotasing's former Roman Catholic church.

Many of Bisco's buildings and churches date from Belaney's days, when the town was also the site of a large lumber mill. But the mill burned during the 1930s and the population plummeted from 250 to fewer than 25. Employment in nearby lumber camps has restored Bisco's number to 50, and during the summer the cottagers who occupy many of the old homes bring it to many times that.

Bisco is a fascinating place to visit. Its remoteness and its collection of churches and old houses perched upon the rocky hilltops at the end of a jarring journey on a woodlands trail (the train is far more comfortable) are the stuff that northern adventures are made of. You can still find the Catholic church sitting precariously on the highest rock, and several simple houses that date from the days of the mill.

You can get to Bisco by train from Sudbury, but you will need a place to stay, for there is no longer a same-day return. In summer and during dry periods, the road is reasonable, though long, and can be reached by following the private E.B. Eddy Ramsay Road (public use is permitted) west from Highway 144 at its junction with Highway 560, 96 kilometres north of Cartier. Then simply follow the arrows. There aren't too many wrong turns in this neck of the woods. Just don't expect to see a sign saying Grey Owl Slept Here.

8

A Touch of the Prairies: Rainy River Country

When crossing the Canadian prairies, you wouldn't bat an eye upon encountering fields of flat black soil and a horizon interrupted by the bulky profiles of grain elevators. You wouldn't expect to find such a landscape in Ontario, the province of forests and rolling pastures, but Rainy River country represents an unusual outlier of prairie Canada right in Ontario.

Tucked into the largely forgotten northwestern corner of the province, Ontario's prairie is guarded at either end by the towns of Fort Frances and Rainy River.

Places like Stratton and Barwick have wooden boom-town storefronts that so typify prairie architecture. Emo's main street faces onto the swirling Rainy River, the state of Minnesota a stone's throw away on the other side.

But the most prairie-like of the towns is Rainy River, located at the western extremity of the plain. Here the wide main street of stores, many now vacant (another prairie characteristic), ends at the railway station. Like most prairie towns, Rainy River was created by the railway, its streets laid out in the usual grid pattern favoured by the railways in their prairie

towns. Because Rainy River was both a divisional point (where a line's locomotives are maintained, crews changed and offices located) as well as a border town, freight yards and grain elevators marked the area around the station.

The station itself was designed by the Canadian Northern Railway, an early line that opened much of the West and built thousands of stations of remarkably similar design. Due to railway modernization, the yards are empty now, the solitary grain elevator soon to be removed. The town has purchased the redundant red-brick station and, with the help of provincial government funds, has converted it into a tourist information office.

Fort Frances, at the plain's eastern extremity, represents the transition between rolling land and prairie flatness. The sight, sound and aroma of pulp mills are far more reminiscent of Northern Ontario. East of the town, the hard rock and the lakes typical of the Canadian Shield landscape stretch uninterrupted to the St. Lawrence River. Yet just west of its town boundary, just beyond the McDonald's restaurant and the Canadian Tire store, Ontario's prairies unexpectedly begin.

Rainy River's prairie-like main street ends at the railway station.

9
Dyer's Dedication: Muskoka's Wilderness Memorial

Calling Muskoka a "wilderness" may be stretching it a bit these days. With lakeside condos and country living, it is now just another area of rural sprawl enhanced by lakes and woodlands. But as you negotiate your car along the ever-narrowing dirt road that leads to the Dyer Memorial north of Huntsville, and the trees on either side seem like an endless forest, you might be forgiven for thinking that it's still a wilderness.

That's what it was when Clifton G. Dyer and his wife, Betsy, began visiting the area. They spent their honeymoon canoeing in Algonquin Park in 1916 and fell in love with the land. In 1940 they built a cottage on the Big East River near Huntsville, returning every year to that wilderness retreat until 1956, when Betsy died.

Dyer was devoted to his wife, and in the years that followed her death he built a moving tribute to her. On the highest point on his property, overlooking their beloved river, he erected a 12-metre stone cairn. He surrounded it with a 390-square-metre flagstone terrace and around that created a 4-hectare botanical garden. On the top of the cairn in a copper urn he placed his wife's ashes to rest. Following his death in 1959, his own ashes were put there as well.

Although the public enjoys free access, Dyer's wilderness memorial is on private property. The Dyer estate, which still maintains the cairn and garden, welcomes visitors, who in the summer may number 200 a day. The memorial is located near the hamlet of Williamsport, about 10 kilometres northeast of Huntsville. Small arrows point the way.

Although Clifton Dyer's cottage was sold long ago, the wilderness memorial to his wife will survive with his dedication to her: "An affectionate, loyal and understanding wife is life's greatest gift."

Dyer's Wilderness Memorial

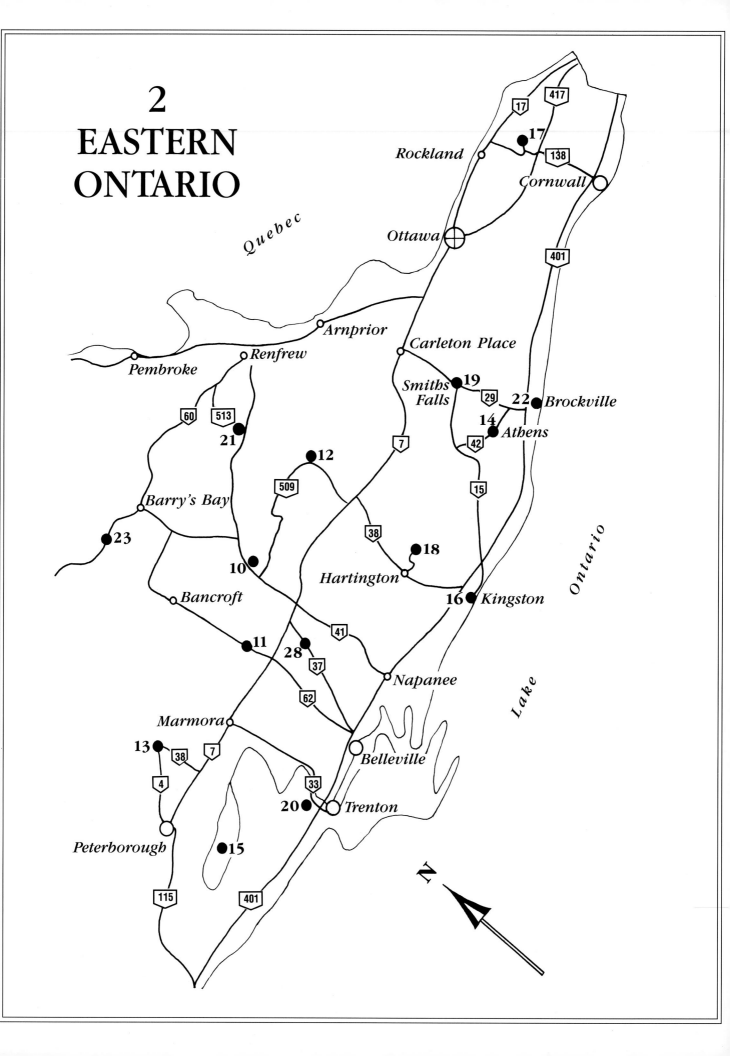

2
EASTERN
ONTARIO

Quebec

Rockland

17

Cornwall

[17]

[417]

[138]

Ottawa

[401]

Arnprior

Carleton Place

Pembroke

Renfrew

Smiths Falls

19

[29]

22 Brockville

[60]

[513]

21

14

Athens

[42]

12

[7]

[509]

[15]

Barry's Bay

23

10

18

Bancroft

Hartington

16 Kingston

Ontario

11

28

[41]

[37]

Napanee

Lake

[62]

Marmora

13

[38]

[7]

[4]

20 •

[33]

Trenton

Belleville

Peterborough

15

N

[115]

[401]

10

Canada's Gibraltar: Bon Echo Rock

Glowing gold and red in the rays of the evening sunset and framed by pine and birch trees, Bon Echo Rock is a ready-made subject for a painting or photograph. Rising for more than 1.6 kilometres straight out of a geological fault line along Mazinaw Lake, this 91-metre cliff has acquired the nickname "Canada's Gibraltar."

Its appeal goes back a long way. For centuries native canoers paused at the foot of the sheer rock face and, using ochre and bear grease, painted their impression of the life they lived and the creatures they revered. Birds, mammals and even human figures are portrayed in what is considered Ontario's largest known collection of pictographs.

The place also appealed to Flora MacDonald Denison. In 1910, Denison, one of Ontario's earliest women's rights advocates, bought the Bon Echo Inn. She transformed the resort into a retreat for Canadian artists and formed the Walt Whitman Club of Bon Echo. For many years the haven drew such artists as Group of Seven painter Franz Johnston, who sketched the cover of Denison's literary magazine, *The Sunset of Bon Echo.*

After Whitman's death in 1919, Flora Denison added what has become the rock's most unusual feature, a tribute to the poet carved into the rock face. In letters a foot high are the words from his poem "Leaves of Grass":

My foothold is tendon'd and mortised in granite
I laugh at what you call dissolution,
And I know the amplitude of time.

The tribute is just north of the narrows that divides Upper and Lower Mazinaw Lake.

Bon Echo Provincial Park was created in 1959 after Flora Denison's son Merrill, English Canada's first important twentieth-century playwright, turned the site over to the Ontario government. It is eastern Ontario's largest provincial park and one of the most popular. Casual campers can drive to one of the more than 500 campsites, and those seeking seclusion can canoe or hike to more remote locations. While rock climbers scale or rappel the sheer granite face, the more passive among us are content to simply stand at the narrows and paint, photograph or just try out the echo of Canada's Gibraltar.

The remarkable Bon Echo Park has been dubbed "Canada's Gibraltar."

11
Ontario's Golden El Dorado

The words "gold rush" conjure images of Barkerville, B.C., or the Klondike, with their boom-town buildings and barroom brawls. They scarely evoke thoughts of Southern Ontario, in particular the rugged hills north of Belleville.

Yet that is exactly where Ontario's first gold rush took place. It all began in 1866, when court clerk and part-time prospector Marcus Powell discovered gold on the farm of John Richardson. One nugget, he wrote, was the size of a butternut.

Once word got out, the rush was on. Grizzled gold seekers streamed in from as far away as Barkerville. In the centre of the gold field, the boom town of El Dorado suddenly appeared. A shanty town of 80 buildings on muddy streets, it was as rough and tumble as any of its western counterparts. When skeptical prospectors, led by the notorious Caribou Cameron, threatened to tear apart some of the mine buildings, 25 mounted police were quickly dispatched to keep order.

They didn't need to stay long, for the gold rush was short-lived. Because the gold was chemically fixed to the parent rock and impossible to mill using existing techniques, the only profit was through fraud. Disillusioned investors salted the claims with imported gold specimens and sold them to unsuspecting greenhorns.

Finally, about the turn of the century, a new milling process allowed extraction to begin and the overgrown mines sprang back to life.

But even their second life was short, for the gold deposits were smaller than was first thought. After a few years of sputtering activity, the mines fell silent and El Dorado became a ghost town. Today its few surviving buildings are occupied once more, and this is a town worth a visit.

Hotels, former stores and even a few of the tiny miners' cabins dot the once-busy network of streets. Of the 80 or so original buildings, only two dozen survive, many with a decidedly boom-town air.

The most interesting structures are at the northern end of the village, where three former hotels sit by the side street that led to the station. Here a historic plaque briefly describes the story of Ontario's first gold rush. The old buildings line Highway 62 about 9 kilometres north of Highway 7.

And what of the old gold camps themselves? Many, with names like Ore Chimney and Star of the East, lie forgotten in the forest, some say with gold yet in the tailings, a hidden treasure just waiting for a Sunday-afternoon prospector to pick up a chunk of ore and echo the word that started the action so long ago, "Gold!"

El Dorado was the site of Ontario's first gold rush.

12

Ride the Rails on the Kick and Push Trail

How many Canadian youngsters have dreamed of looking down on the world from the lofty cab of a train locomotive as the big machine rumbles through forests and across the countryside? For any who have grown up with that yearning unfulfilled, here's something close. It's called the K and P Trail Conservation Area. Probably Ontario's most unusual "park," it follows the railbed of a long-abandoned railway line. And you can follow it in your own car.

In 1883 railway builders opened a line from Kingston to Renfrew. Because its original destination was to be Pembroke, it was named the Kingston & Pembroke or K & P. However, the terrain was so hilly that the wheezing engines could make little headway, and its detractors sarcastically nicknamed it the "Kick and Push."

As was the case with nearly all Southern Ontario's resource railways, its role was soon usurped by roads, and by 1966 most of the northern portion had been abandoned. (Parts of the southern portion lasted another two decades.)

Would-be train engineers can use their cars to follow the former roadbed of the Kingston & Pembroke Railway.

In 1972 the Mississippi Valley Conservation Authority acquired the 40 kilometre portion between Snow Road and Barryvale and opened up the K and P Trail Conservation Area. Park workers cut back the brush, filled in the washouts and generally made the old railbed suitable for cars. Today, during the summer, recreational drivers become would-be train engineers and climb into their "cabs" to follow the railbed that was once the domain of the K & P locomotive engineers.

The route runs from Highway 509, beginning at a point 3 kilometres north of the white church in the picturesque village of Snow Road Station, and winds through lakes and woods to Barryvale, near Highway 511. South of Flower Station, the route passes through a string of historic little villages, the one-time railway towns of Lavant Station and Flower Station, the rugged little former mill town of Clyde Forks and the ghost towns of Wilbur and Folger.

The portion north of Flower Station skirts wide sparkling lakes with names like Flower Lake and Clyde Lake and ends at Calabogie Lake. Although the old causeway across the lake is probably the most scenic section of the old railway line, it cannot be crossed by car.

During the winter months, the K and P Trail becomes the haunt of snowmobilers and skiers, and cars are not permitted.

Because the route has never been accorded the status of road, modern-day "train engineers" should use caution. Some sections may at times be flooded, others washed out. Except for the sites of former railway sidings, the railbed remains as narrow as the railway builders constructed it. When two vehicles approach, one may have to retreat a considerable distance to allow the other to pass.

The K and P Trail offers a unique opportunity to drive an old railway line and dream that dream of sitting behind the throttle of an old puffing steam engine. All aboard!

13

The Disappearing Indian River of Peterborough County

Now you see it, now you don't. After flowing wide and swift through the farmlands of Peterborough County, the Indian River near Peterborough simply disappears.

From its source in Dummer Lake, just south of Stony Lake, it meanders southward until, near the village of Warsaw, it enters an area of limestone. Limestone, as geologists will tell you, is noted for its solubility in water. Water not only erodes limestone but can dissolve it, creating spectacular caves. But water is also able to seep between the porous layers of limestone and seem to disappear. And that's just what the Indian River does.

Normally rivers can flow through areas of limestone and stay in view. The Niagara River does. However, in the vicinity of Warsaw, Ontario, a large outcrop of porous limestone blocks the flow of the river. Rather than go over or around the rock, the river has found enough cracks to simply flow through it.

From the parking lot in the Warsaw Caves Conservation Area, follow a path that leads southeast

The disappearing Indian River.

to the kettles. As you cross the rock fall that blocks the river, you will notice something peculiar: the expanse of fast-flowing water swirls straight into the rocks and disappears.

Beneath your feet you can hear the hollow gurgling as the water makes its way underground. The path continues to another point, where you can see the channel, now dry in the summer, through which the river once ran (and still does in times of heavy rainfall). Finally, after running underground for half a kilometre, the river bubbles back up to the surface to continue its course to Rice Lake.

Near Owen Sound, a much smaller river also disappears underground for a short distance. Ironically it, too, is called the Indian River.

A popular spot for local vacationers, the conservation area also offers a small beach, a picnic area and an unspectacular campground, as well as small but fascinating caves for the cautious explorer. But the river that disappears will provide you with the most vivid memory of this curious place.

14
Main Street Art Gallery: The Athens Murals

Fifteen years ago, the Vancouver Island mill town of Chemainus was on the brink of becoming a ghost town. In desperation, the town commissioned some of Canada's top painters to create murals on the sides of village buildings. The turnaround was spectacular, more than the town had imagined, and today the Chemainus murals have become one of B.C.'s premier tourist attractions.

But you don't need to travel to the West Coast to gaze on such works of art when you can visit Athens, Ontario.

While this attractive little Eastern Ontario town of 1,000 was never in danger of becoming a ghost town, it needed an economic shot in the arm. In 1985, inspired by the success of Chemainus, Reeve John Dancy suggested to council that Athens should celebrate its heritage in a similar way. With financial incentives of $8,000 to $10,000 a mural needed to attract quality artists, the project represented a costly risk. To council's relief, the first three paintings all received rave reviews. By 1992 the main-street gallery had grown to 11 paintings, with a twelfth due in 1993.

Paintings by such artists as Dan Sawatsky, renowned for his work in Chemainus, and Pierre Hardy include *The Gathering*, which depicts residents huddled around a stove to catch up on the local news. A painting of a fire that occurred in 1894 appropriately appears on the wall of the fire hall. One of the most unusual, of the graduating class of 1921, by Sawatsky has a Model T car that appears to be driving right out of the mural.

But perhaps the most popular is that by artist Lorrie Maruscak, a nostalgic depiction of Athens townspeople on the platform of the old railway station welcoming the daily train, a pastime once engaged in by Canadians in nearly every small railway town across the country. Although the station and the tracks have long vanished, it was the building of the

Brockville, Westport & Sault Ste. Marie Railway in the 1880s that gave the town its first economic boost. While the railway was never built beyond Westport, 500 kilometres short of its hoped-for terminus, it did bring limited prosperity to the villages along the way, a prosperity that Athens today hopes to recapture with its murals.

The sign that now welcomes you to Athens pronounces it the Home of the Murals. You can obtain pamphlets from the town hall describing the murals or, during the summer, you can join a guided walking tour.

Athens is on Highway 42 about 10 kilometres west of Highway 29 near Brockville.

Athen's main street murals are rapidly becoming a major tourist attraction.

15
The Rice Lake Railway

As well as its long-vanished stock of rice, Rice Lake is noted for its islands. Known popularly as "whalebacks," these rounded forms are the tops of underwater hills called drumlins by geologists. Sculptured into their smooth whaleback shapes by the glaciers that covered Ontario more than 20,000 years ago, the oblong knolls line up to indicate the direction in which the great ice sheet flowed.

But among these whaleback islands is one that's strangely long and narrow. It owes its origin not to the ice age but to the railway age.

In the early 1850s Ontario's municipalities dropped all pretence at road building and put their money toward the latest transportation craze, the railway. Every town wanted one. Cobourg on Lake Ontario was no different. Its lake port rival, Port Hope, located just 16 kilometres west, had after all just become a busy railway terminus. The railway lines led inland and brought to the port lumber and farm produce, especially barley, for export to the U.S. They also brought prosperity.

Use of the railway causeway over Rice Lake didn't last long.

Cobourg wanted to share in the prosperity and helped finance a railway leading inland. But the Cobourg, Peterborough & Marmora Railway, as it was called, faced an obstacle that the Port Hope line was spared: Rice Lake.

For the railway to detour around the long, narrow lake would have been too costly, so it went straight across it. A combination of a trestle and a causeway seemed to be the best solution, but the railway engineers had not counted on the force of the spring ice floe.

Year after year the ice damaged the trestles, and year after year the railway crews rebuilt them. Then, when the railway was in its tenth year of operation, a particularly strong floe carried off the trestles altogether. Revenues were too paultry to justify rebuilding, and the Rice Lake crossing was abandoned. The only freight worth carrying was iron from the mines farther east, near Marmora, and even that cargo was diverted onto steamers that carried the ore from the lakeside village of Trent River to the railway's new Rice Lake terminus at Harwood.

At the turn of the century the mines closed, and the railway was abandoned south of Rice Lake as well. Stations, rails and ties were all removed. The only evidence, besides the occasional bit of railbed, are the long, thin island and the overgrown causeway that stretches from Harwood into the waters of Rice Lake.

The best views of the old causeway are from the shore of Rice Lake in the village of Harwood (there are some buildings in the village that date from the days of the ill-fated railway) and from the observation platform in the Alnwick Conservation Area a short distance east.

16
Kingston's Little Round Forts

For history lovers, Kingston is Ontario's fun city. With its beautiful stone houses and institutional buildings dating from the 1790s, its historic forts, and two houses where Canada's first prime minister, Sir John A. Macdonald, slept, the city can keep a history buff occupied for weeks. But the structures that cause the most quizzical looks are the little round forts that seem to be almost everywhere.

Named Martello towers after their role in repelling an attack at Cape Mortella on Corsica in 1796, these were the last word in defence. Their small size meant they could be placed in defensive locations otherwise too small for a normal-sized fort. Their circular shape deflected cannon balls, and their high, small windows made them almost impossible to enter. They permitted a flexible line of defence and were almost impregnable.

Of the dozen or so built in Canada (Britain built about 200 worldwide in defence of the Empire), half are in Kingston. Although the oldest were those built in Halifax between 1796 and 1798, those in Kingston were added during the 1840s, when the Oregon Crisis between Canada and the United States once more raised the spectre of the bloody War of 1812.

The military lifespan of the forts in Kingston was relatively short, for in 1860 the newly introduced naval guns had the capacity to demolish the sturdy bastions with a single shot.

Of Canada's surviving Martello towers, those at Kingston, with their red roofs and their neat stonework, are considered the most appealing architecturally. All are readily visible. While two are connected to the museum fortress of Fort Henry, two others, the Murney Tower near Macdonald Park and Fort Frederick tower, are both museums. The third pair, those known as Shoal tower and Cedar Island tower, lie offshore and are accessible only by boat.

Kingston's Martello towers provided a flexible but short-lived line of defence against the Americans.

Death Beneath the Street: Lemieux's Underground Death Trap

As the bus lurched along the winding road to St-Jean-Vianney, a suburb of Jonquière in central Quebec, its wipers smacked vainly at the sheets of rain that lashed the windshield. Suddenly something seemed terribly wrong. Ahead, where the road should have been, lay only darkness. The brakes couldn't hold the slippery black pavement, and the bus slid helplessly into the gaping crater.

Beside the road, the ground buckled and heaved and then gave way, sucking 36 houses and their helpless inhabitants into it.

When the grey dawn finally broke, rescue workers could only gaze in amazement. Where the town once stood, there was now a gaping hole in the ground, a quarter of a kilometre across, and at the bottom a quagmire of watery clay with 31 victims buried in its depths.

The last house in Lemieux.

These innocent men, women and children had fallen victim to an freakish subterranean phenomenon known as "lida clay." A fine sediment, this clay when dry remains deceptively hard and firm, but when it becomes saturated after prolonged rain, it destabilizes and turns to the consistency of quicksand. In thin layers it poses no threat. But a deep deposit can turn without warning into a bottomless quagmire. And that is what happened in the St-Jean-Vianney tragedy.

The dramatic shots on TV and in the newspapers sent soil scientists and planners to their soil maps to identify other areas where the deadly dirt might lurk. One such area lay along the banks of the South Nation River, southeast of Ottawa. Perched on top was the little village of Lemieux.

Lemieux began as a Franco-Ontarian farm village, characterized by the silvery steeple of the Catholic church and the homes and stores huddled at its base. Its future seemed as stable as its past. Then, in the late 1970s, 16 hectares of a nearby pasture collapsed, so soil scientisis decided to act. (Sensing the imminent danger, the cows had stubbornly refused to enter the pasture, as was their daily custom.)

No one could say when the village would be next.

Government geologists warned the population of the deadly menace that lurked beneath them, and in the 1980s began purchasing the village buildings. The last was removed in 1992.

(Post Script: In 1994 the earth shuddered once more, this time closer to home. Less than half a kilometre from the village, an area of land twice the size of the village itself slipped away.)

18

It Came from Outer Space: The Holleford Meteor Crater

Most of us have at one time or another gazed in amazement at the night sky and watched streaks of light. Sometimes many appear in quick succession, and at others agonizing minutes separate them. On rare occasions we can hear the crackle as a "close one" burns up in the atmosphere. These are true visitors from outer space — meteors.

About once a day, somewhere in Canada, a meteor thuds to the earth. Most are only about 100 grams in weight and make little impact, but a few have struck with a tremendous explosion, ripping apart the ground and leaving telltale circular craters or altered minerals.

To date, scientists have recorded about two dozen meteor craters in Canada. The 95-kilometre-wide strike at Sudbury is Canada's largest. The impact of what must have been an enormous meteor was so broad and deep that it completely altered the mineralization of the bedrock and created Canada's greatest nickel deposit.

Of the five meteor craters in Ontario (the others are near Brent in Algonquin Park, at Wanapitei Lake west of Sudbury and at the Slate Islands in Lake Superior), that at Holleford, north of Kingston, is the most visible from the ground.

To reach it, drive to Hartington on Highway 38, about 25 kilometres north of Exit 611 on the 401. From the centre of the village follow the Holleford Road east for 4.7 kilometres. Here it bends left and continues for 3 kilometres to a T intersection. Then, 1.6 kilometres east of the intersection, the road slowly descends a slope. This is the southwest wall of the crater. The road continues east along the slope of the crater for another 0.8 kilometre to the Crater Farm and the ghost hamlet of Holleford, with its weathered old church and community hall.

The best view of the crater is from the pasture just west of the barns on the Crater Farm. The wall of the crater rises to the south behind you and slopes downward to the north to the flat swampland that marks the floor of the pit.

As with most meteor craters in Canada, erosion has softened its features and vegetation covers much of its slope. Yet it is not hard to stand and wonder at how the ground must have shaken when this visitor from outer space thundered to earth.

This crater in the ground occurred when a meteor exploded into the earth's crust.

Smiths Falls's High-Rise Privy

Few of today's generation know much of that grand Canadian institution, the outhouse. Yet for many generations of Canadians that early-morning trek to a frigid outhouse seat was as much a part of everyday life as a warm morning shower is today.

Privies are rare nowadays. But even when they were standard equipment, a two-storey outhouse was almost unheard of, except to Joshua Bates.

In the 1850s Bates, a Smiths Falls miller, chose a site next to his Rideau River grist mill to build a house. No ordinary house, it had some unusual features — an indoor brick bake oven, mirror-image facades and a two-storey outhouse.

The logistics of how a two-storey outhouse might function without unpleasant consequences for the lower occupant are not readily apparent. A closer look, however, solves the riddle. Unlike most, this privy is connected to the house. The structure is wide enough that the upper facility need not be located directly above the lower one. In fact, in the lower chamber a wall separates the seating area from the chute required by the upper facility. While the door to the lower room leads from the downstairs porch, that to the upper room leads from an upstairs hallway. Simple when you think about it.

In 1977 the town purchased the building to use as a museum and restored it to an 1867 appearance. The museum is located on Old Slys Road in the southeast part of Smiths Falls. While you're in town, be sure to visit the beautifully restored Canadian Northern railway station on the west side of the town and perhaps enjoy one of the short rail excursions offered by the railway museum.

At first glance this two-storey outhouse in Smiths Falls defies logic.

20
The Big Boulder

While clawing boulder after boulder from their fields, many farmers have cursed the last ice age, claiming bitterly that all they harvested each year was a new crop of rocks. And they aren't far wrong, for in fields infested with boulders, the freezing and thawing of the ground in the spring in fact squeeze a fresh crop of boulders from beneath the surface.

Most such rocks were deposited during the last ice age, which some scientists claim covered Ontario as much as a kilometre deep. As the ice sheets cracked and began to melt about 20,000 years ago, the torrents of meltwater spewed sand, gravel and rocks into the gaping crevasses. In Central Ontario, the ice sheet melted in a long line, and the glacial debris formed a ridge of rocky and sandy hills. A boulder line that stretches from Orangeville in the west to Trenton in the east was dubbed the Oak Ridges Moraine by geologists.

And it is at Trenton that the ice disgorged its biggest boulder, one the size of a house. Geologists call it the Glen Miller *erratic*, their name for boulders that the ice sheets carried far from their parent bedrock. In Glen Miller, the Trenton suburb where it sits, residents simply call it the Big Boulder.

Despite the young forest that surrounds it, the huge stone towers well above the humbled viewer. Although it sits on private property, it is a spot well visited by residents and tourists alike, who stand in awe at the power of the great sheets that moved it.

The big boulder is behind De Jong's gas station and convenience store on Highway 33, just north of the Glen Miller bridge and 3 kilometres or so north of Highway 401 Exit 525 at Trenton.

Trenton's Big Boulder testifies to the awesome power of the glaciers that covered Ontario during the last ice age.

21
Balaclava: A Real Pioneer Village

It's easy to find pieces of pioneer Ontario that have been moved and preserved in museums, pioneer villages and even on private property. Log cabins, churches and railway stations represent but a few of the many types of structures that await the heritage buff in such locations.

As laudable as these efforts are, the sense of place is lost. A mill belongs beside water, a railway station beside tracks, and hotels, churches and general stores at country crossroads. And that is what makes the hamlet of Balaclava unusual. Located by the sparkling waters of Constant Creek, deep in the hills of Renfrew County, it is a true pioneer village, little altered and on its original site.

Balaclava developed as a mill town on Constant Creek. The first mill was built by Donald Cameron and Duncan Ferguson in 1858 but was operated for nearly a century by the Richardson family before they sold it in 1957 to its present owner, David Dick. The local log supply, however, could serve the mill for only another decade, and in 1967 it closed.

Beside the old mill dam, you can yet see the former blacksmith shop and general store, both still sporting their original clapboard exterior and aging paint.

Below the dam is one of Ontario's oldest water-powered sawmills. Relying on that early form of industrial power, it functioned until the late 1960s, when it was closed down. Sadly, the old structure sags a little more each year and may one day collapse entirely.

Here, too, you can see old barns and a handsome farmhouse right in the middle of town. The best part is that the village has no modern intrusions, no gas stations, no convenience stores. Although the farmhouse remains occupied, the blacksmith and general store long ago shut their doors. Balaclava provides a rare opportunity to see pioneer Ontario as it really was. The place begs to be preserved right where it is, but that has not yet happened.

The village lies along Highway 513, a quiet secondary road north from Highway 132 about 30 kilometres west of the town of Renfrew.

While the buildings are close to the road and easy to see and photograph, they are also on private property, so please don't assume that you can open a door and walk in. To do that, you have to go to one of those preserved places.

The deserted village of Balaclava is a true vestige of pioneer Ontario.

Rails Under Brockville: Canada's Oldest Railway Tunnel

They said, "Every railway has to have a tunnel," so the builders of Ontario's earliest railway, the Brockville & Ottawa, built one.

Until the 1850s, the colonies that would become Canada had relied on muddy pioneer roads and perilous water routes to move people and products. Railways had been operating for two decades in the U.S. and Britain, and in the mid-1850s Canadians decided that it was their turn.

Although the Grand Trunk and the Great Western both began operation in Ontario in the 1850s, neither at that time had a tunnel. The Brockville & Ottawa Railway was designed to link the St. Lawrence River route with Ottawa and to tap the forests and farms between. Because the town of Brockville was built on a ledge of limestone that cut off the waterfront, the railway engineers decided to blast through.

On December 31, 1860, the first wood-burning steam locomotive puffed its way through the darkness, the dim glow from its kerosene headlamp barely illuminating the way. It was Canada's first railway tunnel and the envy of a soon-to-be nation on the verge of the railway era.

But the engineering miracle that was the old Brockville tunnel was later forgotten when, in 1889, the Grand Trunk began digging its 1,800-metre tunnel beneath the St. Clair River, to link Sarnia, Ontario, with Port Huron, Michigan. It marked the first time that tunnel builders used compressed air, and the event was featured in newspapers and engineering journals around the world.

Meanwhile, back at Brockville, the engines of the B & O, and later those of the CPR, continued to rumble through the darkness of the old tunnel.

Gradually traffic to the waterfront dwindled, and in 1970 the spur line was abandoned.

The southern entrance was sealed and the area around it turned into a park. Beside the old oak doors that seal the entrance, a historic plaque tells tourists the tale of Canada's oldest railway tunnel.

Trains once rambled under the town of Brockville to reach this tunnel.

23
Wilderness Ruins: The Madawaska Roundhouse

What makes ruins in Ontario so interesting is that there are so few of them. Many that survive have been stabilized and preserved for historical interpretation. Those that lie in out-of-the-way places, unknown to all except a few area residents, are the most fascinating, because they are often unaltered and unexpected. For example, you just don't expect to find the ruins of a massive railway roundhouse in a place like Madawaska.

Madawaska is a much smaller place than it was when the railway came to town a century ago. Canada's millionaire lumber king John Rudolphus Booth was busy building his Ottawa, Arnprior & Parry Sound Railway to Georgian Bay, and Madawaska was conveniently located for a divisional point with its services and supervisors.

At such locations, passengers of the day would have seen a large station, often with a restaurant, employee housing, a large expanse of sidings where trains are made up, and a roundhouse. The roundhouse was usually the most massive of the structures at a divisional point. Its round walls encircled a turntable that would pivot the locomotive towards whatever bay it needed for maintenance.

Booth's line was a busy one. With the grain port of Depot Harbour at its west end, and with Booth's timber limits in the the park itself, it was not unusual to see trains puff through Madawaska at 20-minute intervals. Then, in 1933, a trestle in Algonquin Park was damaged and the owner, CN Rail, decided not to repair it, in effect severing the line. The line west of Algonquin Park (from Scotia Junction to Depot Harbour) was abandoned in the late '30s and early '40s. Train service into the park continued until the late '50s, while east of the park the line was abandoned in stages and today ends at Renfrew.

You can find many remnants of Booth's old line. The railbed through Algonquin Park is used by lumber trucks, and that near Parry Sound is maintained as a snowmobile trail. In the town of Barry's Bay, the railway station and water tower are preserved as reminders of the town's busy lumber days. Meanwhile, exposed to the winds of Georgian Bay, Depot Harbour has become a popular and fascinating ghost-town destination. The railway swing bridge to it now carries only cars.

(Post Script: Sadly, in 1994, these magnificent ruins were removed.)

Ruins of a railway roundhouse lurk in the woods near the village of Madawaska.

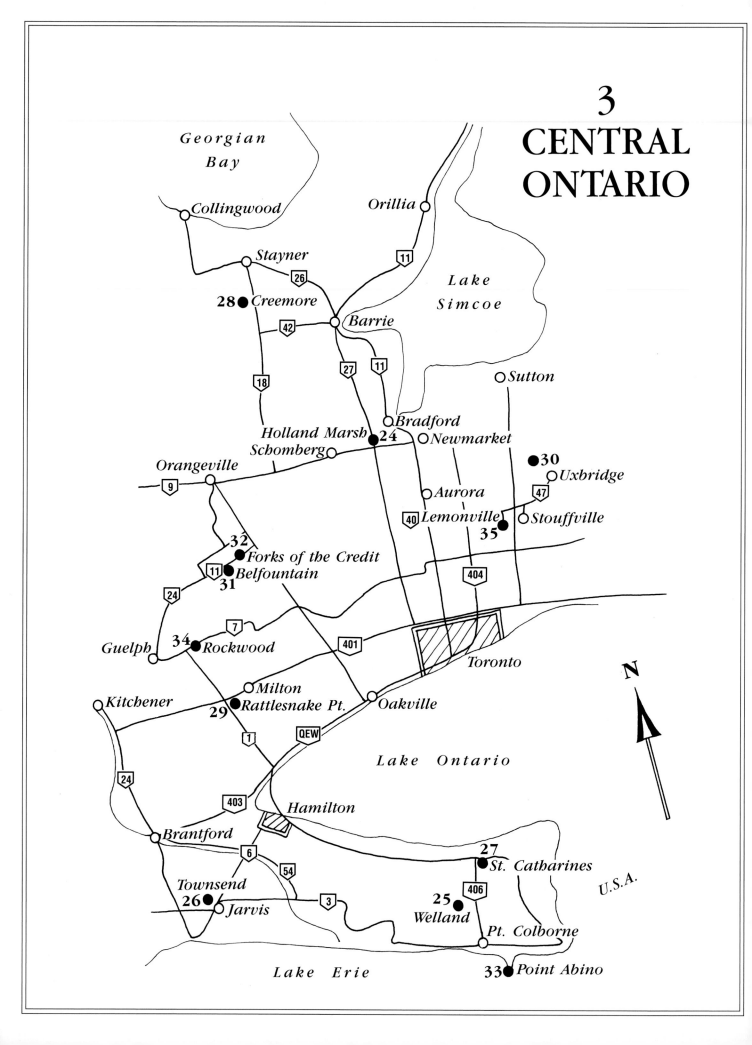

Georgian Bay

○ *Collingwood*

○ *Orillia*

○ *Stayner*

[26]

Lake Simcoe

28● *Creemore*

[42] ○ *Barrie*

[27] [11]

[18]

○ *Sutton*

○ *Bradford*

Holland Marsh ●24

Schomberg ○ ○ *Newmarket*

● 30

○ *Orangeville* ○ *Uxbridge*

[9]

○ *Aurora*

[47]

[40] *Lemonville* ○ *Stouffville*

35●

32● *Forks of the Credit*

[11] ● *Belfountain*

31

[24]

[7] [404]

Guelph 34● *Rockwood*

[401]

Toronto

N

○ *Milton*

Kitchener ○ ● *Rattlesnake Pt.*

29 ○ *Oakville*

[1] [QEW]

Lake Ontario

[24]

[403]

Hamilton

○ *Brantford*

27

[6] ●*St. Catharines*

[54]

Townsend

26● [3] 25● [406]

○ *Jarvis* ●*Welland*

U.S.A.

○ *Pt. Colborne*

Lake Erie

33●*Point Abino*

25
The Comfort Giant: Canada's Biggest Maple Tree

A specimen of the tree that symbolizes Canada may be older than the nation itself.

The Comfort Maple squats wide and solid beside a field near Welland, Ontario. It was there in 1816 when the Comfort clan first settled the land, and has remained there since, its survival defying all the odds.

Ontario once boasted a magnificent forest cover. Oak, hemlock, beech and maple provided a cooling leafy canopy that assured a high water table, which in turn allowed the many rivers and streams to flow year-round, cascading into streams that powered the countless pioneer mills. But that forest quickly vanished. What fires and old age didn't claim, pioneer wood-hewers did.

With the forest gone, the water table lowered and the streams dried, turning the once-vibrant mill towns into ghost towns. But the Comfort Maple survived.

With its girth of 8 metres and crown width of 28 metres, the 30-metre-high giant became a local attraction, and owner Earl Hampton Comfort set aside a piece of land solely for the preservation of his tree. In 1961 his sister Edna donated the tree and .4 hectare of land around it to the Niagara Region Conservation Authority.

The tree sits just east of Regional Road 28, about 2 kilometres north of Highway 20 near Welland, Ontario. And it probably will for a long time to come, a tribute to a pioneer family and their love for Ontario's natural heritage.

The Comfort Maple is said to be Canada's largest maple tree.

24

The Swamp That Feeds the World: The Amazing Holland Marsh

Like much that is unusual and interesting in Ontario, the Holland Marsh is paid scant attention by travellers. To most, the marsh is little more than flat black fields that flash past as they propel their cars along Highway 400. Yet for the driver who slows down and exits the 400 at Canal Road, the marsh becomes one of the most interesting bits of landscape not just in Ontario but in Canada.

It is the country's largest vegetable garden.

That wasn't the case around the turn of the century, when this post-glacial lake bed with decayed plants 30 metres deep was good for little else than growing marsh grasses to stuff mattresses.

Then, in 1904, a Bradford grocer named Watson convinced professor W.H. Day of the Ontario Agricultural College in Guelph to investigate the possibility of draining the swamp for vegetable production. All studies and experiments pointed to the same thing — the swamp could become one of Canada's premier market-garden areas.

In 1925 the Ontario Department of Agriculture began to drain the bog. Canals and dikes enclosed both sides of the valley like huge brackets, diverting the water to Lake Simcoe. In 1930 the waters of the former Holland River were contained within the two canals, and the rich black soil was drained and ready for farming. The first farmers to arrive were 18 Dutch families in 1934 and '35. Many others, including Russians and Poles, followed and within a few years the one-time swamp had become one of North America's leading vegetable-producing areas. (The name Holland Marsh does not come from the Dutch settlers but rather from Maj. A. Holland, who surveyed the land in 1830.)

Canal Road, which skirts the northern rim of the marsh, provides the best look at the 2,900 hectare marsh. From the tree-covered portion that surrounds the intersection of Highway 9 and Canal Road, the road follows the northerly of the two canals through a seemingly southern world of overhanging willows and still canal water. It passes modern backsplits, older bungalows and the tiny cabins that house the seasonal workers who arrive each year to pick the lettuce, potatoes, celery, parsnips, cabbage, cauliflower and 120,000 tonnes of carrots.

Although many of the original farm homes were destroyed during the devastating floods brought by Hurricane Hazel in 1954, the Dutch village of Ansnorveldt, tucked into the southeastern corner of the marsh, with its rows of small houses resembling Dutch ones, remains largely intact.

Canal Road continues to a junction with Highway 11 in Bradford. Here vegetable markets offer shoppers and back-road travellers some of the freshest produce they will find anywhere.

From Highway 11, swamp grasses take over the landscape for the 8 or 10 kilometres to the marsh's confluence with Lake Simcoe. Scanlon Creek Conservation Area north of Bradford affords a view of how much of the marsh may have appeared before it was transformed.

OVERLEAF:
The Holland Marsh

26
The Townsend Experiment

There is something peculiar about Townsend. As you drive along Highway 3 west from the attractive small town of Jarvis about 50 kilometres south of Hamilton, you see the signs. They point down what is at first glance a side road and advertise lots for sale in a place called Townsend.

After you drive a short distance down that side road, passing fields and barns as you travel, you suddenly find yourself on a four-lane boulevard. Branching off to the sides are streets that twist and curve, lined with modern houses. Farther on, you find a sleek seniors' accommodation, and a town complex centre overlooking a pond. And then Townsend ends as abruptly as it began.

But look more closely. You will find that those suburban streets end in overgrown fields, that the avenues are strangely free of traffic and that the town centre contains little more than drab government offices.

Welcome to Townsend, once touted as Ontario's grand community of the future. In the 1970s government planners decided that the sprawl engulfing the Toronto-Hamilton-Oshawa area was out of control and should be redirected to a series of regional growth centres. The decentralization, theorized the planners, would also help spread the prosperity of those boom years to less populated and less prosperous regions.

The planners chose an area of flat farmland near the shores of Lake Erie to build a modern and planned new town. The land was far enough from Toronto to be relatively cheap, yet close enough to benefit industry. By 1976 coloured maps showed a proposed community of 100,000, with areas for recreation, housing and industry. The curving streets would lead to a mix of housing types, while tree-lined trails would welcome hikers, cyclists, horseback riders and cross-country skiers. There would be high schools, hospitals and supermarkets, all connected by public transit.

But at the centre of it all would be the community showcase, the town centre. Built overlooking a landscaped pond, the centre would contain four department stores, specialty shops, restaurants, churches, cinemas, an art gallery and a hotel. An apartment complex would house 6,000 residents, and sports lovers from throughout the region would travel to the stadium and sports fields. The first phase would start in 1978 and accommodate 5,000 people.

But somehow the dream city turned into a nightmare. When the Canadian economy plunged into its dreadful recession and inflation skyrocketed, industry stayed away. So did most of the 100,000 future residents.

In fact, Townsend never expanded beyond that first phase. The recreation trails are overgrown, no buses rumble along the streets, and the town centre contains only a drugstore, a post office and social service offices. The grandly named Town Centre Road ends appropriately in an overgrown farm field.

Down by the lake, where the industrial park was to be, there stands a Stelco steel plant and the Nanticoke generating station. Although these complexes provide jobs for hundreds of area residents, most commute from their original homes and have never bothered to relocate to Townsend.

While Townsend is no ghost town and looks much like any other well-maintained suburb, the sudden dead ends, the silence, and the town's odd location in the midst of fields and barns are all evidence that the "dream city" never came true.

The partially finished new town of Townsend.

St. Catharines's Forgotten Tunnel

St. Catharines, Ontario, is the place for ship-watchers. Built as part of the St. Lawrence Seaway, the Welland Canal cuts straight through the city. Although the lift bridges provide long, frustrating waits for commuters, the canal is a delight for boat buffs, who, while drivers fume, enjoy watching the huge ships inch by. (Serious boatwatchers usually head for the public Lock Three viewing area.)

St. Catharines is also a bonanza for history enthusiasts, for it is home not just to the current Welland Canal but to three predecessor canals, as well. Throughout the city, trails and bicycle paths lead past the old stone locks and canals, reminders of an era when the largest schooners could fit crossways on a modern vessel and were pulled through the canal by horses.

The first Welland Canal was opened in 1829; the third canal was replaced in 1930 by much of the fourth, the current, canal. Many of the old canal structures are well indicated in heritage hiking brochures, but one of the hidden treasures of the old canal age is the long-abandoned Grand Trunk Railway tunnel beneath the third Welland Canal.

Built between 1875 and 1881, it lasted less than 20 years and was replaced by a bridge over the canal. Today it lies forgotten and uncelebrated, saved by a few die-hard history enthusiasts, behind a tangle of trees, and in the darkness only a trickle of water passes where steam locomotives once puffed. The graceful limestone arch that marks the entrance is a lasting monument to the workmanship of the railway builders of the past century.

You can drive to the path that leads to the tunnel by following the Seaway Haulage Road south for 2 kilometres from Glendale Road in the eastern end of St. Catharines. From the guardrail on the western side of the road, a path leads into the ravine and the forgotten tunnel.

In the pond on the eastern side of the road, you will also find some of the long-abandoned lock structures of the third canal itself.

St. Catharines's forgotten railway tunnel is part of its seaway legacy.

28
The Battle Over the Smallest Jails

Usually people fight over who has the biggest, the best or the fastest. In this case, what's contested is who has the smallest — the smallest jailhouse in Canada, that is.

The contestants are the towns of Tweed, situated 40 kilometres north of Belleville, and Creemore, 25 kilometres west of Barrie.

Tweed, on the northwest shore of Stoco Lake, is mainly a tourist town. Its long and narrow main street dates from the time when it was a busy railway junction, when the Canadian Pacific Railway and the Bay of Quinte Railway crossed at approximately the middle of town. Both lines have been removed, and the only vestige of that forgotten era is the former CPR station, now a lumberyard office.

At the south end of the main street sits a small stone building. Built in 1899, the three-cell jail operated until 1950, when a new facility opened. The jail was more likely to contain homeless migrants, displaced by the Depression and in need of a warm shelter, than any hooligans. This, Tweed residents proudly proclaim, is North America's smallest jailhouse. Measuring only 4.8 by 6 metres, this tiny treasure could be just that.

But don't make that claim in Creemore. A bright and prosperous farm town with wide tree-lined residential streets, it, too, has "North America's smallest jail," or so they say. Constructed in 1892 with three cells, this jail welcomed miscreants until the 1940s. One block east of the main street, and just behind the library, the flat-roofed stone structure measures just 4.5 by 6 metres. The building is not open for public viewing unless its owners are on the premises, but a commemorative plaque assures visitors that this is not just Canada's but North America's smallest tank.

It looks as if Creemore comes up the winner, but the dimensions are so close that maybe the contest can be considered a tie.

Fortunately for miscreants, neither facility has maintained its original use. The Creemore jail is simply closed, and that in Tweed is a tourist office. But wait a minute — there's a little jail in Port Dalhousie, near St. Catharines, that supporters now claim is the smallest...

Perhaps it's better not to reveal to either community that in a remote ghost town called Berens Rivers, a once-bustling gold-mining community isolated in the remote northwestern Ontario bushland, sits a single-cell hoosegow really no bigger than a privy, considerably smaller than either of the two "smallest" jails in Canada.

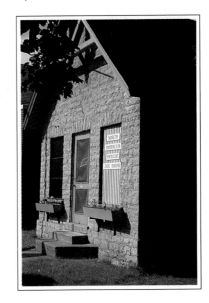

Which jail is the smallest, that in Creemore (above) or that in Tweed (right)?

29
Ontario's Oldest Trees

Think of an old-growth forest and you think of redwood trees that soar upward until their tops disappear in a canopy of green. You don't envisage gnarly little cedars that twist out of the side of a rock and only 3 or 4 metres into the air. Yet these spindly little survivors are Ontario's oldest trees.

Normally a swamp species, the eastern white cedars are found along the lip of the Niagara Escarpment and some of them date back more than 600 years. Dating such a tree is not an easy job. It requires boring into the trunk and then counting, often with the aid of a microscope, the hundreds of nearly invisible rings concentrated into the span of a hand.

From seeds that lodged in the limestone crevices centuries ago, the saplings slowly edged outward from the side of the cuesta and then bent upward to face the warm and nutritious sunlight.

Anchored in the stony depths, with no soil to feed them, the trees grew imperceptibly. But at least they grew. Their difficult location, on the side of the cliff, spared them from loggers, farmers and browsing animals, and even from encroachment from other tree species. While original forests were falling all across Canada, the sturdy little white cedars sat firm and continued their slow growth skyward.

They are easy to see, but not to identify. Thanks to recent planning, much of the Niagara Escarpment is finally open to the public. One of the best sites to view the ancient trees is in the conservation area at Rattlesnake Point. A short path leads from the farthest parking area to the trail along the brink. The stone fence protects careless walkers from a dangerous and likely fatal tumble over the precipice and also allows

Ontario's oldest trees are also among its smallest.

an easy view of the old trees. They can be identified by their light-green flat cedar needles and by their trademark origin in the side of the cliff face. But as for the age of those that you see, only a bore sample and a tedious tally of the tiny rings can tell you if the tree is 60 or 600 years old.

Some experts believe that too much public use might threaten the future of this old-growth forest. However, an interpretation area would not only help today's generation to understand this unusual part of Ontario's natural history, but would also protect the more vulnerable forest areas from curiosity seekers.

30
Ontario's Taj Mahal: The Thomas Foster Memorial

You don't need to spend a lot of time looking for this one; it dominates the countryside on County Road 1 about 2 kilometres north of Uxbridge.

Thomas Foster, a former Toronto mayor and parliamentarian, was in his 70s when he decided to tour the world. While visiting India, he gazed in wonder at the beautiful Taj Mahal, built in 1628 by Shah Jahan as a monument to his wife, Mumtaz Mahal. Foster decided he, too, would build a Taj-like temple for his own wife. The location he chose was a hilltop just north of Uxbridge and not far from his old home town of Leaskdale.

Defying the Depression, Foster hired European workmen to fashion the limestone temple. The workers cleared away the hilltop and then began carefully laying limestone and marble according to the intricate plan. When they were done, the strange Byzantine monument rose more than 18 metres into the air. The onion dome, built of copper, allowed the sun to filter through 12 stained-glass windows. The coloured rays fell upon marble mosaics, lighting up the pinks, greens and blacks that depict such mythological scenes as the River Styx and Alpha and Omega. The cost eventually exceeded $200,000, a personal extravagance almost unheard of in those hard times.

In the centre of the monument, Foster placed a marble altar that contained the remains of his wife, Elizabeth, and later those of his daughter Ruby, who died in 1945 at the age of 10.

While the spectacle is easily viewed and photographed from the road, visiting is limited to just a few summer Sundays and is under the auspices of the local museum.

Thomas Foster modelled his memorial to his wife after India's Taj Mahal.

31
Belfountain Park: The Stamp Man's Legacy

Under the gaze of a small cannon, the west branch of the Credit River plunges over a 10-metre waterfall and then tumbles down a rocky canyon. Beside the cannon are winding pathways lined with elaborate stonework, a chapel-like cave with the name Yellowstone, and a stone fountain with a bell on top.

This is the Belfountain Conservation Area, the creation of millionaire philanthropist Charles W. Mack. It is one of Ontario's more interesting parks.

Better known as the industrialist who invented and then manufactured the cushion stamp, Mack purchased this property on the rocky bank of the Credit River in 1908. By the tumbling waters, he built a summer home for himself and his wife, and they named it Luck-e-nuf. He then hired master landscaper Sam Brock to create a park.

When finished, Brock had created a wonderland in stone. His park contained a dam for swimming, a lookout point, and a cave that he had converted into a chapel-like room.

Beautiful Belfountain Park was once a private estate

He had slung a swing bridge across the canyon and topped it all with a stone fountain with a bell on top, to commemorate the name of the village.

Belfountain, which straddles the canyon rim, began in 1825 as a pioneer settlement named McCurdy's Village. During the 1860s it became the home to mining company executives who managed the stone quarries in the Credit canyon below. By the time Mack showed up, the mines had closed and the miners' villages of Brimstone and Forks of the Credit had become ghost towns.

But Mack's park was quite popular, for when he had finished his park he opened it to the public. People could come to picnic, hike or swim, provided that they obeyed Charles Mack's rules: no swimming on Sundays, men were to wear swim tops and women skirts at all times.

After Mack's death in 1943, his park was sold and operated as a commercial business until 1959, when the Credit Valley Conservation Authority purchased the property. Additional acquisitions between 1961 and 1973 have given the grounds more space for picnicking, longer hiking trails and indoor washrooms.

Although Mack's modest cottage and cabin are now only foundations, most of Brock's handiwork remains in place. You can look into the Yellowstone cave, watch the waterfall from the lookout, cross the canyon on a newer swing bridge, or simply sit by the fountain with the bell on top.

The Forks of the Credit: Another World

In a province better known for its farms, woodlands and rolling hills, the Forks of the Credit area is a world apart.

One of Central Ontario's largest rivers, the Credit, begins in the Orangeville area as two tributaries. After tumbling their way through fields and forests, the two branches suddenly begin a precipitous plunge down two different canyons. Finally they meet, their foaming rapids leaping into one wide river.

Above this watery junction, the walls of the canyon tower more than 100 metres into the air, a defile that continues downstream until the walls part and then widen to continue both north and south as the Niagara Escarpment.

Not surprisingly, the Credit Canyon has become the enclave of dozens of wealthy home owners who have tucked their mansions into the rocky hillsides or perched them prominently on the clifftops.

The vestiges of earlier activities also linger on the landscape. During the nineteenth century, the area was a major producer of construction stone. Several noisy quarries clanged away on the cliffs, producing beautiful stones for such buildings as Toronto's Old City Hall and the provincial legislature buildings. The workers built their simple cabins in villages like Forks of the Credit and Brimstone on the valley floor, while the more affluent managers inhabited the airier clifftop town of Belfountain.

Although newer homes have replaced many of the old village houses, you can still find a few workers' cabins in Brimstone and at the site of the Forks of the Credit village. Here, Southern Ontario's longest and highest railway trestle looms above the roadway.

The scenery at the Forks of the Credit is unlike any other in Southern Ontario.

The road to the canyon is, with little question, the most spectacular in Southern Ontario. As you follow the Forks of the Credit Road west from Highway 10, you soon begin to see the high cliffs of

the Niagara Escarpment in the distance. After a few sharp twists and turns, you find the Credit River bubbling along beside you. Finally, by the bridge that leads north to Brimstone, you can park. On the south side, a fine new log home marks the dead-end road that leads to the old Forks of the Credit village site. The only surviving buildings are an original house and a school.

The road to Brimstone is now also a dead end, but it was once a busy route that followed the north branch of the river to the village of Cataract. Today it remains busy, with Bruce Trail hikers.

As you pause in the canyon, you can picnic by the river, follow the Bruce Trail south beyond the Forks of the Credit village or north past Brimstone. The remnants of a long-abandoned lime kiln lie just off the Bruce Trail to the south, and the large ruins of once-prosperous Daigle grist mill await you at Cataract, to the north. Although many of the sites lie within the newly created Forks of the Credit Provincial Park, parking is confined to just a few locations, most of them inconvenient.

After the road passes under the railway trestle, it suddenly lurches right and then left in an unexpectedly sharp hairpin turn. After this dramatic finale, the hillsides begin to level out, and one of Ontario's most scenic driving experiences is behind you.

Guiding Light: The Beautiful Point Abino Lighthouse

Perhaps it's because most of them lie on isolated shorelines, often out of view of most landlubbers, that lighthouses are among the least appreciated of Ontario's heritage structures.

Some are small and squat, made of wood; others are tall and elegant, constructed of stone or brick. Then there is the lighthouse at Point Abino. Built of poured concrete, it is unlike any other lighthouse in Ontario. Constructed in a form of architecture more in keeping with grand urban structures, it is easily the most elegant lighthouse along the Ontario side of the Great Lakes. Its style has to do with the neighbourhood.

Point Abino is located on Lake Erie just west of Fort Erie. With the urban boom that engulfed Southern Ontario and upper New York state at the turn of the century, increasing numbers of city dwellers sought out the beaches and breezes of the nearest lakeshores. These numbers swelled following the opening of the Peace Bridge between Buffalo and Fort Erie in 1927. More modest cottages and cabins crowded the beaches in nearby Crystal Beach, but the forested peninsula at Point Abino became the exclusive enclave of wealthy industrialists. Families from New York and Ohio, like the Rich family, owners of Rich Products, and the Baird family, owners of the *Buffalo News*, erected huge summer homes there.

In 1918 the federal government replaced the old lighthouse with a structure that, with its smooth white finish and its sweeping lines, resembles a Spanish mission rather than a traditional lighthouse.

That's not to say that Ontario's other lighthouses are not worth visiting. During the late 1800s the government built around the shores of Lake Huron half a dozen lofty stone structures that they termed the Imperial Towers, probably because of their height. Of the six, the one at Cape Rich near Southampton is the most accessible. The squat stone lighthouse from the Duck Islands has been moved to the Mariners Museum near Picton, Ontario. Port Rowan lays claim to having Ontario's oldest wooden lighthouse.

Although no lighthouse in Ontario remains permanently staffed, most are still in use, their mercury vapour lights now operated electrically. For that reason, lighthouses have largely been spared the kind of rampant demolition that brought down most of Ontario's old railway stations.

Even if the Point Abino lighthouse is Ontario's most interesting, it is not that easy to visit. The access road is a private thoroughfare for the cottage community, and outsiders are generally not permitted on it. Fortunately, the lighthouse lies close to local boat-launching facilities, so landlubbers willing to make the effort by water can discover one of the hidden treasures of the Great Lakes.

The Point Abino lighthouse is easily the most elegant on the Ontario shores of the Great Lakes.

34
Rockwood's Potholes

Most communities don't like to brag about their potholes, especially when they're 6 metres wide and 12 metres deep and number almost 200. Rockwood, Ontario, about 12 kilometres northeast of Guelph, is different. Residents not only boast of their potholes but have created a park for them.

The reason for this pride is that the potholes are not a result of neglected roads but are a fascinating creation of nature.

Sedimentary rocks such as limestone or sandstone are among nature's softest. Easily eroded, they can be sculptured and washed by wind and water into a fairyland of shapes. Caves, natural bridges and rock pillars are but a few of the shapes that the rock can assume.

Potholes are another form, occurring when boulders become trapped in the swirling eddies of fast-flowing rivers. As the boulders swirl round they make a hole in the bedrock beneath. Thousands of years must pass for the rocks to create a hole even the size of a stew pot. Tens of thousands of years were required to form those at Rockwood.

The natural wonder is preserved in the Rockwood Conservation Area on the western outskirts of the town. Trails lead from the parking lot up cliffs, past caves, even beside the ruins of a huge stone grist mill and around the potholes themselves. Here the Eramosa River flows through a watery labyrinth of potholes, some of which have collapsed, others eroded through. Other potholes remain high and dry and lurk darkly beneath the vegetation.

The most interesting way to see them is to rent a canoe and coast lazily through the watery maze. You'll see potholes as you've never seen them before.

Rockwood's potholes

The Floating Mansions of Lemonville

It's a watery wonderland, but one that's a long way from any river or lake.

Lemonville sits on the slope of a sandy hill, the grey apartment towers and suburban glass offices of northeastern Toronto looming on the hazy horizon. An undistinguished hamlet that dates from pioneer days, Lemonville has in the past 20 years seen a most unusual housing boom, mansions that float on water — or so they appear.

The water comes not from a river or a lake but from a massive and mysterious underground reservoir. The ridge that looms behind the mansions is known as the Oak Ridges Moraine. A line of sandy hills, it was formed when the great glaciers that once covered Ontario cracked and began to melt. The icy meltwater carried sand and rock into a long fissure in the ice, and by the time the glacier had melted, all that remained was the long ridge.

Because the soil in the hills is so porous, rainwater drains right through it, causing a high water table at the foot of the hills. That is not unusual, but the Lemonville area sits on a geological anomaly. While the water seeps quickly through the light sandy upper soils of the ridge, the flow suddenly meets a hard subsurface layer of clay. This propels it even faster towards the flats below and keeps the water near the surface, like a massive underground lake, held down only by the soil above it. Because of the downward force of the water in the hills behind, whenever the surface of the flats is broken, the water gushes upward like a geyser unleashed.

House builders turned what could have been a curse into a blessing. By digging carefully into the underground lake, they have landscaped the large housing lots into miniature lakelands. Surrounded by ponds, some more than .8 hectare in area, are mansions in styles that range from California ranch to Woodbridge Italianate, or simply to Scarborough suburban. So popular are the little lakes that house prices in excess of $1 million are not unknown.

The land of the floating mansions extends south on McCowan Road for about a kilometre from Bethesda Road and 2 kilometres west along Bethesda Road to Kennedy Road. Vacant lots and survey stakes along the roads promise that there will soon be more floating mansions.

Lemonville's mansions are set in a watery wonderland.

4
TORONTO'S
NOOKS & CRANNIES

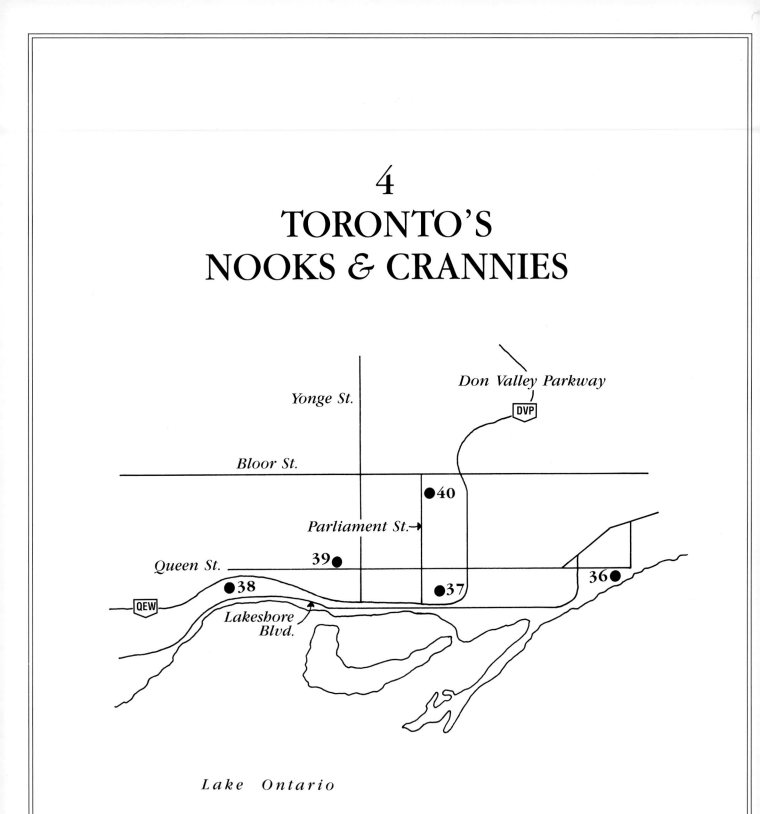

36

The R.C. Harris Filtration Plant

In the east end of Toronto, on a grassy slope overlooking Lake Ontario, sits one of the city's most attractive and least known buildings.

No wonder. It's a water treatment plant.

Such facilities seldom inspire much interest. But this one is different, and its difference is attributed to its magnificent architectural style.

The R.C. Harris plant was built in the 1930s to treat water for what was, until the Depression, Toronto's booming eastern outskirts. It was named after Rowland Cole Harris, head of Toronto's public works department, a man who appreciated grand public buildings. The style that Harris chose for this building was art deco, an attractive modern style in vogue during the 1920s and '30s, and often used for skyscrapers and other grand buildings of the day.

Another noteworthy example of art deco is the former Toronto, Hamilton & Buffalo Railway station and office building just off James Street in downtown Hamilton. Canada's only railway station built entirely in this style is shortly to reopen as Hamilton's new GO Transit station.

Characterized by streamlined curves and shapes, art deco is also a style that was relatively short-lived. After the Second World War, the tastes of a generation turned against the recent past, the years of war and the Depression. Architects began to favour austere buildings of concrete and glass.

Several tours of the Harris plant are available on weekends, and times are posted at the entrance. Some of the stylistic treatment inside is as interesting as that outside. Besides the filtration process itself, you can see the marble interior of the Filtration Hall, the turbine and water motifs carved into the limestone of the lower pump building. Outside the building, you can wander the spacious grassy grounds or stroll along the Lake Ontario's gravel beach.

The R.C. Harris Filtration Plant is located on Queen Street East, at Neville, the eastern terminus of the Queen streetcar line. That popular stretch of Toronto's shoreline known as The Beach, with its parks and its famous boardwalk, lies immediately to the west. And as you watch the waves lap in, you realize that after having toured the plant, you at least have a better understanding of what comes from the lake.

The art deco R.C. Harris sewage treatment plant.

37
An Industrial Survivor:
The Gooderham and Worts Complex

Despite a history of insensitive and often unnecessary demolition, Toronto can still claim a remarkable collection of heritage buildings. While structures like the Old City Hall, Casa Loma, Trinity Church and Simpson's are widely known, those less famous are just as compelling and are often more so.

Paramount among Toronto's forgotten heritage is the Gooderham and Worts complex at Trinity and Mill streets. It is perhaps Canada's oldest and most complete early-nineteenth-century industrial complex.

In the 1830s English miller James Worts chose the confluence of the Don River with the harbour to erect a wind-powered flour mill, eastern Toronto's first industry. He was later joined by his brother-in-law, William Gooderham. It was common in pioneer Canada to use industrial by-products for secondary industrial operations, so Gooderham and Worts used the second-grade grain from the mill to operate a distillery.

In the 1850s the Great Western and Grand Trunk railways completed their lines into Toronto, and the waterfront boomed with industry. In 1859 Gooderham and Worts added a magnificent limestone distillery, the beginning of an expansion phase that lasted intil 1890. By 1861 the company was producing 6,000 gallons of whisky a day, and by 1870 was responsible for one-third of Canada's rye whisky production. Extensive sections of the waterfront were filled in, and soon the plant was nowhere near the lake. Access to water transport was no longer needed once the railways were in operation.

In 1927 the firm merged with Hiram Walker of Windsor, and the Gooderham and Worts facility became a secondary production plant. In 1986 it was purchased by Allied Lyons of England. Four years later it was declared obsolete and closed, after a century and a half of liquor production.

Because it had been relegated to a lesser role in its later years, the entire complex was little altered and remained much as it appeared in the 1890s. Its size and age make it one of Canada's most remarkable historic industrial complexes, and it has been declared a national historic site as well as a candidate for UNESCO heritage classification.

Yet its future remains uncertain, for it lies right in the path of downtown Toronto's eastern growth. The buildings have been the site of art displays and could enjoy new life as an arts centre of some type.

Tours of the interior are not available, except when exhibits are on display, but the magnificent exterior is easy to see. The buildings cover a four-block area between Parliament and Cherry streets, south of Eastern Avenue, and are familiar to drivers on the Gardiner Expressway. Among the several structures in the complex are the slender Italianate cupola and the old limestone distillery building.

Despite its magnificence, the complex is still little appreciated other than by vagrants, film companies and a small but growing number of heritage enthusiasts who are now discovering that Ontario's industrial heritage is every bit as beautiful as its castles and its city halls.

The Gooderham and Worts industrial complex, a candidate for world heritage designation.

38
Ode to Joy:
The Last Joy Gas Station

Architecture and gas stations just don't seem to go together. Mention the latter and one thinks of gas pumps, the smell of old oil and a building whose architecture is better left undiscussed.

But that wasn't the case during the 1920s and '30s, when the auto was popular and gas stations quickly became part of the neighbourhood landscape. While price wars and gimmicks were the most common forms of competition, one method, undertaken first by the Hercules Oil Company of Detroit, was to create an attractive style of gas station.

Ironically, the style that Hercules chose was that which had been introduced more than 30 years earlier by the CPR when their railway stations were designed to attract passengers to their rail service. Known as the chateau style, it incorporated steep bell-cast roofs and high towers. The Joy Oil Company introduced them to Toronto in 1937 and, with their high red roofs and white stucco siding, these mini-chateaux soon became landmarks in many areas of the city.

Following the war, architectural styles changed. North America wanted to forget the dark years of war and the Depression that preceded it. Decorative features such as turrets and steep roofs were discarded in favour of the airiness and simplicity of flat roofs and large windows.

The last Joy gas station is a relic from another era.

Cars became bigger and soon clogged the streets and the growing network of highways. To keep up, the gas stations needed to be larger and more efficient. The tiny Joy gas stations were inadequate to meet the demands of the auto age. Corporate image was important, too, and the subsequent owners of the Joy stations replaced them with the newest styles.

The old Joy gas stations quickly began to disappear from the landscape. By the mid-1980s only four remained in Toronto, and by 1992, there was just one. Located on the north side of Lakeshore Boulevard just west of High Park, this solitary survivor was built while the Queen Elizabeth Way was under construction. Twenty years before the Gardiner Expressway opened, Lakeshore Road was the main access to the QEW, and a location on this busy thoroughfare was profitable for any gas station or motel.

In 1989 the last Joy gas station, now owned by the OLCO Petroleum Group, was designated by Toronto city council as a heritage structure worthy of preservation. With the development pressures that Toronto is experiencing, the designation does not guarantee the building's survival. For the moment it stands as a lonely reminder of a time when the car craze was in its infancy. The six lanes of traffic that roar past it today indicate that much has changed since then.

39
The Feeling of Being Watched: Toronto's Old City Hall Gargoyles

Have you ever had the feeling that you're being watched? Stand in front of Toronto's Old City Hall, and you are. By the gargoyles.

Old City Hall is a remarkable example of the Victorian Romanesque Revival architectural style. Completed in 1899, it was one of those grand municipal buildings typical of the period. With its tall clock tower dominating Bay Street, every nook and cranny — and there are many — of its sandstone exterior seems to offer a different architectural surprise.

Especially the gargoyles. While such grotesque faces were common on medieval buildings, some of those on Old City Hall carried a special meaning. City Hall architect E.J. Lennox had staked much of his reputation on what he hoped would be his masterpiece. But when the Toronto city councillors of the day shortchanged him, or so he thought, he decided to even the score. There, above the grand entrance, sits E.J. Lennox's revenge: the gargoyles are the distorted faces of the councillors. In a final act of defiance, Lennox added, contrary to instructions, his own name and a caricature said to resemble himself.

Old City Hall is festooned with dozens of the more traditional gargoyles, grotesque animal-like faces, but the faces of the Toronto council of the day will live on in a way none had likely intended.

Much of Victorian Toronto has vanished. Fine old buildings of stone or brick have fallen victim to insensitive redevelopment and builders whose bottom line doesn't include a respect for heritage. Even the Old City Hall itself was threatened when the Eaton Centre was proposed.

Amid modern glass-and-concrete towers, the gargoyles of Toronto's Old City Hall still keep watch.

The faces of Old City Hall.

Toronto's Wellesley Cottages

Toronto's little nooks and crannies hide many surprises. While old and architecturally more splendid buildings are widely known, smaller and simpler structures are often even more interesting because their odds of surviving demolition or alteration are comparatively slim.

That's the case of Cabbagetown's tiny Wellesley Cottages located just north of Wellesley Street at Sackville. During the 1870s and '80s, Ontario's railway boom years, labourers' cottages, as they were called, were hastily built to house the influx of workers. Between then and the 1890s, thousands were constructed in working-class neighbourhoods all across Toronto. The Wellesley Cottages were built about 1886–87.

Constructed of wood, usually with no foundation, these tiny one-and-a-half-storey cabins all boasted a centre plan and many a trademark gable over the front door. The style earned its designers an architectural award for workmens' cottage design at the Crystal Palace exhibit in England in 1851.

Over the years, demands for bigger and safer housing meant the end of a housing era in Toronto and the gradual disappearance of these simple abodes. Throughout the city, only a few isolated examples survive. The Wellesley Cottages are a remarkable row of seven. They are located not on a residential street but on a tiny lane behind the back yards of the principal row of houses.

After a time as low-cost rental units, they were sold to a developer who upgraded them, a trend in Cabbagetown, which since the 1970s has become gentrified.

Much of old Cabbagetown is equally interesting. A stroll along Wellesley, Sumach (Cabbagetown old-timers pronounce it ''shoo-mack''), Spruce and Winchester streets reveals a residential neighbourhood of small houses that date from the days when the area's low-income residents planted cabbages in their front yards, giving the community its unusual name. In this area you will also find the former Riverdale Zoo, now an animal farm for children, and the Spruce Court apartments, built in 1913 as Toronto's first government-sponsored housing project.

A few blocks to the south, in an area of Cabbagetown replaced in the late 1940s by low-cost apartments, is Toronto's ''smallest'' house. Built about 1885, 383 Shuter Street is a mere 2.5 metres wide. It was a single-storey dwelling until 1981, when extra floors were added. If basketball great Wilt Chamberlain were to lie crossways in it, he would have no room to stretch.

AT TOP: *Toronto's tiny Wellesley cottages.*

AT LEFT: *Labourers' cottages built in the late 1800s.*

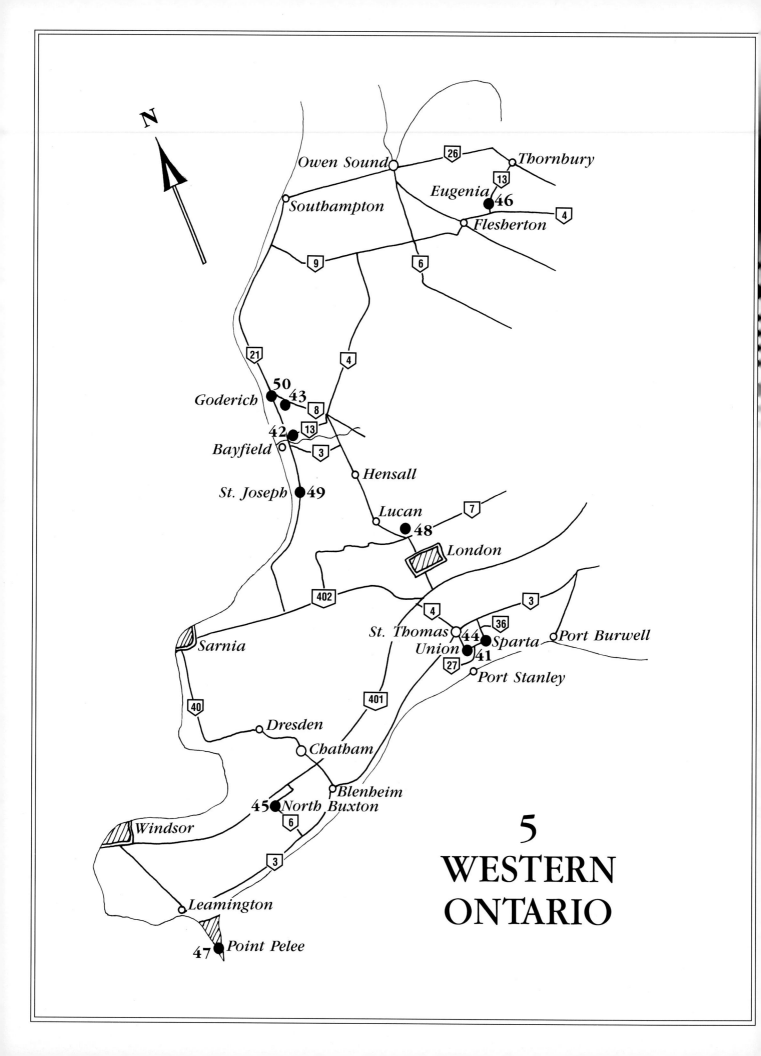

41
A Quaker State: Sparta Village

One of the best preserved and most unusual villages in southwestern Ontario is tiny Sparta. The name Sparta is apt, for the village was founded by a band of frugal Quakers. The first arrivals in 1813 flirted with danger, as the War of 1812 was still raging; and with Yankee raiders on the alert to penetrate Ontario's vulnerable southwest, homes and mills could quickly be put to the torch.

While the war raged all around the Great Lakes, Sparta was spared. In 1823 it was formally established as a Quaker settlement and in 1832 adopted the name Sparta. Until then it had been simply The Corners.

Southwestern Ontario contains Canada's most fertile farmland, and Sparta prospered. Between 1840 and 1880 the main street boasted a hotel, a general store, a tailor, a glovemaker, a cheese factory and three cabinet shops. A combined flour and grist mill rumbled on nearby Mill Creek until the clearing of the forests so depleted the water table that the little creek carried too little water to power the heavy millstones.

Sparta's unusual adobe blacksmith shop.

Sparta lacked only one important thing — a railway. As the railway era swept Ontario in the 1870s and '80s, Sparta's businesses could no longer compete with those in communities with a railway line and a station. Growth stagnated. Sparta remained suspended in time.

What many residents of the day may have considered a curse is seen today as a blessing. Stores, houses and shops that stood 150 years ago still stand today, little altered, and they have made Sparta a popular destination for heritage lovers.

A walk down Main Street will take you past some of Ontario's oldest and most unusual village buildings. Clustered about the main intersection are the Sparta Peddlar, a general store dating from 1846. The Village Tea Room is kitty-corner, in the old Sparta House hotel, and across from it is the Temperance House, built in the 1840s.

But among Sparta's many aging houses and stores, two buildings stand out, unusual not because of their age, although both date from around 1827-30, but because of their construction. Both are made of adobe, bricks made of clay and straw, a rarity outside of the American Southwest. They are located on Main Street, just steps west of the main intersection. One, the blacksmith shop, is on the north side of the street close to the centre of town, while the other, the Mud Cottage, sits farther west on the south side of the street.

Sparta nestles at the junction of Elgin County roads 27 and 36, about 15 kilometres southeast of St. Thomas, Ontario.

42

A Touch of Holland: The Bayfield Windmill

A field of tall grass bends before the warm summer winds. Above the field four huge wooden wind sails creak in a slow circles. They belong to North America's only wind-powered saw- and grist mill.

Frank de Jong is descended from generations of Dutch millers. Wind-powered sawmills, though rare in Canada, are part of his family heritage and remained in his blood when he migrated to Canada following the Second World War. When he purchased a parcel of land beside the Bayfield River southeast of Goderich, Ontario, he set about to recreate his own touch of Holland, a saw- and grist mill that would be powered by wind alone. Eighteen years went into creating the mill pond, 13 into the mill.

When it was finished, the mill, wind cap and sails towered 29 metres above the flat Bayfield River marshlands.

Although the mill is privately owned, the de Jongs have provided ample facilities for visitors, and indeed encourage them.

For a society accustomed to the sometimes ceaseless roar of gas engines, the sounds of the mill are a welcome relief. The creaking of the sails and the grinding of the blades sound refreshingly natural. On the main floor of the mill, cable and hooks drag the logs onto the slipway, where they are pulled slowly forward to the saw blades. These can number from 2 to 12, depending on the desired width of the cut lumber. Above the mill, a balcony encircles the wind cap. Above that are the four 22-metre wind sails that creak in the wind.

Inside, trained staff explain how the sails can be positioned to face the wind and how the rotation of the huge sails alone operates the saw- and the grist mill.

In the visitor centre, separated from the mill by a bridge, visitors can learn the history of the mill from a video or enjoy a quick bite from the small snack bar. Nearby, the Mill Side House provides bed-and-breakfast accommodation for those planning a longer stay in the area.

And the area offers plenty to see, from the beautiful and busy tree-lined main street of Bayfield to the strange circular main street of Goderich and the vanished main street of the ghost town of St. Joseph.

The windmill is located south of Huron County Road 13 about 3 kilometres east of Highway 21. Look for the green arrows that point the way to The Windmill, Ontario's touch of Holland. (Open to the public between May and October.)

Bayfield's wind-powered sawmill.

43

Carved in Stone: The Apple Park Farm Statues

If you stop to buy apple cider, apple butter or even plain old apples at the Apple Park Farm, don't be surprised if you get the feeling that you are being watched. Surrounding this attractive brick farmhouse on Highway 89 east of Goderich are more than 50 stone figures, many of them comic, that depict pioneer life in early Ontario.

George Laithwaite moved to the farm from nearby Holmesville in 1895, and for the next 60 years he carved from local limestone caricatures of people and depictions of scenes that he saw around him.

In pioneer Ontario, with no radio or TV shows to sap the imagination, reading the Bible was a popular pastime. Accordingly, Laithwaite drew from the Scriptures for his sculpture of a lion with a lamb and of the Queen of Sheba. He satirized politicians with his portrayal of Sir John A. Macdonald and Sir Robert Borden turning swords into ploughshares. The more raucous aspects of pioneer life appear in the caricatures of a drunken farmhand

staggering home supported by his braying donkey, and in four drunken fishermen tottering home from a "fishing" trip.

Early travellers to Goderich soon began to go out of their way to see Laithewaite's sculptures, and at one point they were so popular that Laithewaite built a visitors' centre and sold postcards.

His grandson, Edward, did not carry on his grandfather's passion for sculpting when he took over the farm in 1955. However, he cares deeply for the statues and welcomes guests to stroll in the property at their leisure and gaze in admiration at one of the more unusual legacies of pioneer Ontario. Although postcards are no longer available, visitors can select apple cider or apple butter from the shop on the farm.

A postscript: Time is sadly taking its toll on the limestone statues. Weathering and acid rain are wearing away the humorous, the gentle and the exaggerated features. Without some government help to preserve them, this legacy will gradually vanish.

One of the more rollicking of the Park Farm statues.

44
The Smallest Union Station

What is the size of a two-hole outhouse and attracts tourists from across the continent? The answer is North America's smallest Union Station.

In railway terminology, a "union" station is shared by more than one railway company at a time. More often than not they are large urban terminals. Therefore, when train travellers think of Union Station, they picture the high-vaulted concourse of Toronto's Union Station, or the beautiful Roman arches of that in Washington, D.C. They are not likely to envisage the tiny grey flag station that guards the track of the Port Stanley Terminal Railway. Its name derives not from its size or its function but simply from the name of a nearby hamlet.

Not only is it the oldest building on the once-busy line, but the style and the arched windows reveal that railway architects paid as much attention to the tiny flag stations as they did to the larger, more elegant city stations.

The Port Stanley Terminal Railway was resurrected as a labour of love from the ruins of the pioneering London & Port Stanley Railway. Originally built to carry lumber and farm products from the southwestern farmlands to the port at Port Stanley, it eventually became an excursion line. Londoners

The flag station at Union, still in use, is North America's smallest "union" station.

crowded into the coaches at the now long-demolished brick-and-stone station to go to the beaches or to dance to the big bands that played the internationally renowned Stork Club.

Eventually CN took over the line and, after a few years of dwindling traffic, closed it. While other stations were demolished, the little flag station at Union was given little thought. When the line was eventually abandoned, Union Station, deteriorating and overgrown, miraculously still stood.

Local rail enthusiasts purchased the line and, after pouring countless hours and money from their own pockets into its repair, have restored passenger rides from Port Stanley through Union to St. Thomas.

Awaiting the passengers is the smallest Union Station, restored, repainted and housing old photos and railway memorabilia.

You can board the excursion trains at the decidedly larger station in Port Stanley and travel the few miles up the line to Union, or, if the trains aren't operating that day, you can follow the Golf Club Road west from Highway 4 in Union.

45

Ontario's Deep South: The Black Heritage of Buxton

Of all the fascinating aspects of Ontario's varied history, one that remains relatively unknown is the story of Ontario's black settlements.

As in the American South, early Ontario settlers accepted slavery as an institution. Many wealthier households had slaves. Only the absence of a labour-intensive system, like the plantation system of the American South, kept the numbers low.

Trading in slaves was banned by Britain in 1808, but slavery itself continued until 1832. Three more decades passed before the practice was finally abolished in the United States.

During that period, American abolitionists helped the slaves slip their bonds and follow the Underground Railroad to Canada and freedom. Throughout Ontario, many societies sprang up to help the escaped slaves to establish new lives.

The 140-year-old schoolhouse in North Buxton recalls the area's black heritage.

One of these was the Elgin Settlement at Buxton in Southwestern Ontario. It was founded in 1849 by Irish Presbyterian missionary William King, who had himself inherited 15 slaves in Louisiana through marriage, slaves whom he soon released. The Elgin Settlement was unique. Rather than owning the land in common, the usual practice in such settlements, each settler could acquire his own parcel. Lots were 50 acres each and cost $2.50 an acre. Houses had to be 18 x 24 feet in size and set back 33 feet from the road. The settlement quickly grew to 2,000 and, with its saw- and grist mill, potash factory, brickyard, hotel and various stores, was considered Ontario's most successful settlement of ex-slaves. Although the abolition of slavery in the U.S. in 1863 drew many black settlers back south, the Elgin Settlement survived. Today 98 percent of Buxton's residents trace their roots to ancestors who settled the area as ex-slaves.

Sadly, other Deep South attitudes also survived. Public school segregation, for example, existed in a nearby town until the 1960s, and during the same decade a restaurant owner in another town steadfastly refused to serve blacks.

Buxton's black heritage makes it an unusual and fascinating place to visit. The best place to start is with the Raleigh Township Centennial Museum in North Buxton, about 15 kilometres south of Chatham.

A pleasant modern building, it contains archives and artifacts from the earliest days of the Elgin Settlement. A nearby school dates from 1861, and a Methodist church and cemetery from 1855. Across the road sits an original settlement homestead that the museum hopes to acquire, though government funding cutbacks have now made that a more distant dream.

Buxton's businesses, like those in most Ontario communities of its size, have moved to larger centres, leaving part of the area uninhabited. Even the former railway station sits vacant behind large bushes.

The Hole in the Hill: The Mystery of the Eugenia Arches

Dry most of the year, and unheard of by most Ontario travellers, Eugenia Falls in the Beaver Valley has been the site of some strange activities.

In the 1850s a case of mistaken identity led to a short-lived gold rush. Mistaking the shiny lustre of iron pyrite for gold, a party of would-be prospectors sparked a flurry of digging and panning until more knowledgeable assessors assured all that the mineral was only fools' gold.

The next venture was more practical. In the 1870s William Hogg from Hogg's Hollow just north of Toronto bought land adjacent to the falls and built a small electric plant to provide power to a few local communities.

Buoyed by his success, Hogg went back to Toronto to try to sell city officials power for their expanding streetcar system. The Adam Beck plant at Niagara Falls was closer and more reliable, so Toronto's politicians sent a dejected Hogg back to Eugenia.

In 1903 a group of Toronto businessmen formed the Georgian Bay Power Company and tried once again to capitalize on the questionable power potential of Eugenia Falls. To maximize the drop, they decided to build a tunnel through the hill beside the falls to the bottom of the valley far below.

They began digging the tunnel in 1906, but unexpected problems with quicksand pushed the cost to over $1 million. By 1907 the tunnel was finished.

The entrance to the long-lost tunnel at Eugenia.

At 867 feet (264 m) long, 9 feet (2.7 m) high and 8 1/2 feet (2.6 m) wide, it was big enough to drive a buggy through. And someone did just that.

Perhaps it was pride of workmanship, but the distinguishing feature of the tunnels was the beautiful stone arch at either end, described by some as "Roman" in appearance.

But the plant never did operate and the tunnel remained dry. Instead, a dam was built at Eugenia Lake itself, from which an even greater and more reliable fall of water could supply a larger plant built farther down the Beaver Valley.

Although the tunnels themselves have long collapsed, the arches have withstood weathering and erosion. They are located in the Eugenia Falls Conservation Area in the village of Eugenia, just south of Thornbury. The larger and more complete of the two arches stands near the brink of the falls on the opposite side of the river from the walking path. (For safety reasons the conservation authority has posted the river, though it is dry most of the season and the flat limestone riverbed is more like a sidewalk.) The second arch has collapsed and can be found only after a long and steep hike, and a bit of luck.

The little wooded park is a hikers' paradise, though it has few facilities beyond a trail along the canyon rim and a washroom. Look on the stone walkway for a name carved into the stone in 1903.

Point Pelee: Where Canada Begins

Stand here and all of Canada is north of you. So, for that matter, is much of California.

At 42° north latitude, Point Pelee is the most southerly part of mainland Canada and lies south of much of the continental United States, including Northern California. Such a southern latitude also provides the point with a range of southern vegetation found nowhere else in the country, vegetation more common, in fact, to the Carolinas. Even prickly pear cactus is found there. Indeed, the rare plant and animal life earned the point its status as one of Canada's first national parks.

But its history goes back far beyond that. Owing to Point Pelee's strategic location well into Lake Erie and close to American shipping lanes, the British military in the 1790s set the point aside as a naval reserve. That didn't stop a handful of squatters, known as "Pointers," from moving in and starting up fishing and small-time farming.

The sandy soil limited the range of crops, and the point gradually became more popular with hunters and birdwatchers. Then, in 1918, through the efforts of ornithologist Percy Taverner and his bird-lover friend Jack Miner (founder of the nearby Jack Miner Bird Sanctuary), the government of Canada designated the reserve as a national park, one of Canada's first. Commercial fishing operations persisted until the last lease expired in 1969, and a few cottagers hung around even after that.

Nature lovers now arrive from around the world to look at prickly pear cactus or such rare plants as

Point Pelee is Canada's most southerly point of land.

the burning bush and the butterfly weed; birds such as the prothontory warblers and white-eyed vireo; or the spectacular fall migration of the beautiful monarch butterfly, during which branches of trees are entirely enveloped in orange butterflies.

Park planners have made the park's many features easy to see. Boardwalks guide nature lovers through the vast marshes, and pathways lead them to the cactus patch; even one of the old squatter shacks has been preserved for history buffs.

The most unusual experience in the park is the point itself. After the trees end, a bare sand spit leads another 1.25 kilometres into the lake. (This, some believe, gave the point its name, the word *pelee* meaning ''bald'' or ''peeled'' in French.) The point narrows until it becomes a pencil point and then fades beneath the waves. But you can walk beyond even that into the shallow waters of Lake Erie and look back on Canada — all of it.

The Telltale Grave: The Donnelly Tombstone

It's okay to go to Lucan these days and talk about the Donnellys. Few among today's generation are familiar with that name, but a century ago all North America knew about the Black Donnellys. On a bitterly cold night in February 1880 a local vigilante gang attacked their homes and brutally butchered five of their number. Members of several prominent local families stood trial for the grizzly slaughter, among them the sheriff, and a horrified world followed the macabre details in the newspapers. The first trial resulted in a hung jury. In the second, the judge instructed the jury to disregard the testimony of a young eyewitness and the accused vigilantes went free.

The massacre was the result of an ancient Irish feud and a bitter business rivalry, all played out in an era when drunkenness and violence were part of pioneer life. Eventually the feud reached such a fever pitch that beatings and burnings became routine, and many of them were blamed on the large Donnelly clan. On February 4, 1880, 40 vigilantes swept down on two houses occupied by the Donnellys and murdered the five. Daily newspaper reports of the trial kept the English-speaking world transfixed for months.

In the 1950s the legend spawned a colourful paperback account of the bitter feud. Other books and even plays followed, but in Lucan the memories were slow to fade and any mention of the Donnellys was frostily rebuffed.

Lucan is one of those down-to-earth farming towns where many still trace their roots back to the first pioneers. Several had grandparents or great-grandparents who were part of the simmering feud, and a few were part of the vigilante gang.

Today time and perhaps celebrity have combined to ease, if not altogether erase, the bitterness. Residents will now direct you to the famous Roman Line, where the clan lived, now less colourfully called Concession 6, located between Lucan and Elginfield on Highway 4. (Some may even offer to sell you a souvenir Donnelly baseball cap or T-shirt.)

All evidence of the old Donnelly homestead has long vanished, as has the little schoolhouse where the vigilantes plotted their heinous crime, but the old St. Patrick's Roman Catholic church still dominates the inter-section as it has since the days when the Donnellys first arrived.

The Donnelly tombstone still sees many visitors.

Behind the church, in the graveyard, it all comes home: A simple marble headstone lists several members of the Donnelly family. What is striking are the five deaths dated February 4, 1880.

The original stone, long removed, was boldly emblazoned with the word "murdered." Today's stone simply says "died."

Field of Dreams: The Story of St. Joseph

Narcisse Cantin was a dreamer. Born to French-Canadian parents on the shores of Lake Huron near Goderich, Ontario, Cantin was, by the age of 17, a cattle shipper. On his many trips to Buffalo, he met several business friends and witnessed firsthand the remarkable economic boom that the Erie Canal had brought to Buffalo and indeed to all of upper New York state.

Why, he wondered, couldn't such a transformation happen to Southwestern Ontario. About 1900 he began to lobby the federal government to build a canal. A precursor to today's St. Lawrence Seaway, it would bypass the longer Detroit River route and cut from Lake Erie straight across Ontario's southwestern peninsula to Lake Huron.

While the government dithered, Cantin acted. He assembled a huge tract of land near his proposed Lake Huron entry and named his townsite St. Joseph. He then convinced a number of his Buffalo associates to establish businesses in St. Joseph. He populated his town with 25 families of French-Canadian émigrés in Michigan.

The jewel in his crown would be his hotel. Four storeys high and topped with two towers, it would have the longest bar in North America and was touted as a four-seasons lakeside mecca.

Two of St. Joseph's few remaining structures.

But a political scandal and the First World War intervened to crush his hopes for a canal. Businesses folded and the hotel was eventually demolished. It had stood for more than 20 years and never opened its doors. Many of the settlers moved away, and much of St. Joseph disappeared from the landscape.

Today the site of Cantin's hotel, the businesses and his would-be canal sit in an overgrown field, a field of dreams. A provincial historical plaque commemorating the dreamer himself stands beside the foundation of the ill-fated hotel, while many of the remaining village "streets" are now little more than dirt tracks. Here and there a few of St. Joseph's grand homes still stand, strangely out of place at the otherwise quiet country crossroads. One of them, belonging to Napoleon Cantin, houses historical documents relating to Narcisse Cantin's efforts.

Many Ontario ghost towns harbour the broken dreams of the men and women who had hoped for a better life for themselves and their families, but nowhere did the hopes of a city depend so completely on the dreams of one man, and nowhere were those dreams so completely dashed as at St. Joseph.

The site lies 37 kilometres south of Goderich at the intersections of Highways 21 and 84.

Going Round in Circles: Goderich's Eight-Sided Main Street

If you spend any time driving on Goderich's main street, you soon get the sense that you've been there before. That's because you are going around in circles. Goderich has an unusual main street. Designed to accommodate the convergence of eight radiating streets onto a market square, it is a perfect octagon. In fact, the only other city in North America that was planned that way is Washington, D.C., and even that pattern was later altered by the imposition of a grid street pattern.

Goderich's eight-sided main street has remained intact. It was designed by John Galt, the first commissioner of the Canada Company, a pioneer land settlement company, who wanted the town that was his headquarters to be unique. Drawing on the city-planning concepts of Roman architect Marcus Pollio Vitruvius, he laid his eight-sided town down in the uncleared forests of pioneer Ontario. Few other examples of the style exist anywhere in the world, and none as exact as Goderich's.

Some theorize that Galt goofed and that the plan was originally intended for the town eventually named after Galt himself. The city of Galt, after all, was the jump-off point for the Canada Company settlers. Galt's inland location was more suited to radial growth, while Goderich, on Lake Huron, could spread unencumbered on only half the routes.

But it was just such a lakeside location that sparked Goderich's growth. With the arrival of the Buffalo, Brantford & Goderich Railway in 1858, and in 1908 the Guelph & Goderich, the town boomed even more. A grand courthouse replaced the market in the centre of the square in 1856, and hotels and stores of yellow brick filled in the eight sides.

Goderich's eight-sided main street was based on an early Roman town plan by architect Marcus Pollio Vitruvius.

Although much has been lost to fires and insensitive redevelopment, a number of the outstanding buildings have survived. One of the most imposing is the three-storey Bedford Hotel, built in 1896, and located between South and Kingston

streets. With its corner entrance and its magnificent domed roof, it suits its corner location and visually dominates that side of the square. Between Kingston and East streets stands the former Victoria Opera House. Built in 1887 it is characterized by high arching windows on the second and third storeys.

With funds from the Ontario government, the town and the business community have improved and upgraded the appearance of the square with brick sidewalks, new streetlights, and benches and planters.

Goderich has more to offer the heritage enthusiast besides the square. The unusual eight-sided jailhouse, located north of the square on Victoria Street, is now a museum. West Street leads to the lake and takes you past the Port of Goderich town hall.

Once at the lake, you will see the former CPR railway station with its strange-looking ''witch's hat'' roof above what was the waiting room. The CPR has removed its tracks and the building is now owned by the municipality.

Another railway station, this one in use, sits four blocks east of the square at the corner of East and Maitland. This former CNR station, with two attractive towers, has been taken over by the short-line Goderich & Exeter Railway. The success of this little line with what was once a money-losing branch of CN Rail proves that bigger isn't necessarily better.

Goderich does indeed have much to offer visitors, once they stop going around in circles and figure out how to get off that darned eight-sided main street.

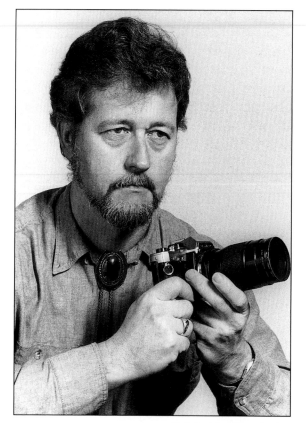

photo by Adam Photo Services

In his relentless quest for the unusual and the offbeat, writer, photographer and latter-day explorer Ron Brown has probed nearly every nook and back road in Ontario. In his many publications on ghost towns and back-road attractions, and in his frequent radio guest spots, he has shared his discoveries. His university background in geography and planning brought out the explorer early and he has spent much of the last quarter century on dusty roads and forest trails. And he is far from finished. There are many bends in the road that beckon yet.

Dear Reader:

We hope you've enjoyed this book. We hope you've enjoyed it enough to tell us some of the strange and wonderful things you've seen in your travels around Ontario. Please write to us at the address below. If we use your ideas in the next volume we'll give you credit and send a free book upon publication. Thanks.

> *More Unusual*
> c/o The Boston Mills Press
> 132 Main Street
> Erin, Ontario
> N0B 1T0